Grandpa Hikes the Pacific Crest Trail

*To Dan,
With appreciation...
Jim and Zhita Rea*

Jim and Zhita Rea

ISBN: 9780692837443

Cover photo of authors by unknown friend, other photo, map and images by Jim Rea. Front cover photo on PCT in North Cascades in Washington, descending north toward Canada.

Over the Hill
Long Beach, CA
jimrea77@gmail.com

ISBN: 0692837442

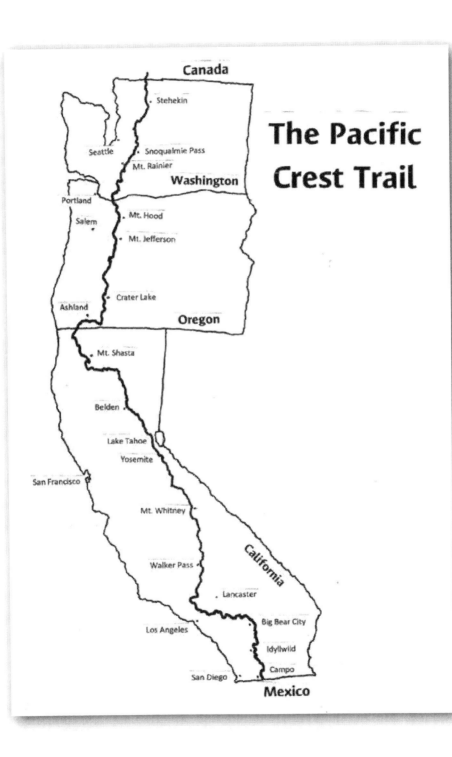

The Pacific Crest Trail

Canada

Stehekin

Seattle

Snoqualmie Pass

Mt. Rainier

Washington

Portland

Mt. Hood

Salem

Mt. Jefferson

Crater Lake

Ashland

Oregon

Mt. Shasta

Belden

Lake Tahoe

Yosemite

San Francisco

Mt. Whitney

California

Walker Pass

Lancaster

Big Bear City

Los Angeles

Idyllwild

San Diego

Campo

Mexico

Acknowledgements

This is the story of a wonderful adventure, an experience that was made possible by Zhita, my beloved wife, partner and support team. I can't imagine being able to enjoy the experiences I had in this venture without her generous and enthusiastic and loving participation. The reader will see how she sought out and created opportunities to adventure alongside me. We learned together how best to develop our teamwork in challenging circumstances, with few precedents we knew to guide us. Other hikers who learned about the way she teamed up with me were naturally very envious. Her memories, notes, writing and editing were essential to the completed story in this book.

The participation, encouragement, and support of many others among our family and friends greatly enriched the adventure. Hiking with my brother John Rea, my daughters Darbi Gill and Kirsten Rea, and my grandsons Sawyer and Tanner Gill provided cherished experiences; hiking with Susan Wanser and many other friends was both enabling and rewarding. Much of this will be evident in this story, and more can readily be imagined from the many references to hiking together, welcome respites from hiking, and visits in the homes of family and friends.

I first learned about training for a hike from Susan Le Sage, a fitness trainer who expanded her repertoire to include backpacking. She organized the Barefoot Sage outdoor club, which I joined in 2001 when I was 65 in preparation for a 2002 hike in the Grand Canyon. In addition to the key concept of training for a hike, Susan also initiated club members into learning about good equipment, nutritious food, hike planning, checklists and much more. She was an inspiring mentor. When I discovered how much I enjoyed hiking, I also joined Susan in taking a class from Wilderness Medical Associates to learn about first aid, in addition to enrolling in a training program for Grand Canyon hike leaders.

I owe much to the eye-opening experience of participating in a Memoir Writing Workshop led by Samantha Dunn with UCLA Extension in November, 2013. I enrolled when I was in the midst of writing a sort of journal account of my hike. I felt I was presented with a nourishing stew of new ideas and perspectives in the workshop, and I scooped what I could into my porous burlap sack of a brain, unsure what would remain as I returned to writing the story. Samantha and other workshop participants drew me out of a more pedestrian (couldn't resist) approach to the story, to the benefit of my family and other readers.

We prize the fresh perspective and editing help of my daughter, Darbi Gill.

I wrote a shorter version of the rescue story which was published by Mountaineers Books in 2011 in the Pacific Crest Trailside Reader, Oregon and Washington. Our revised account of the rescue appears in Over the Hill with permission from Mountaineers Books.

The font or typeface for place names on the map is Massif Pro, a trademark of Monotype Imaging. Massif was designed by Steve Matteson. He drew the letters by hand, basing his design, in part, on sketches he drew of Half Dome while backpacking in Yosemite.

Contents

For Zhita, my wife, partner and support team.
Her participation makes this
adventure tale also a love story.

Over the Hill

Grandpa Hikes the Pacific Crest Trail

JIM AND ZHITA REA

We have two or three great experiences in our lives –
experiences so great and moving that it doesn't seem
at the time that anyone else has been so caught
up and pounded and dazzled and astonished and
beaten and broken and rescued and illuminated and
rewarded and humbled in just that way ever before.

F. SCOTT FITZGERALD

Retirement

If there is not an abundance of time, then let us
cherish the abundance of things we have that
make time precious. Dancing and music and
hiking and work and friendship and love.

RUTH LAMPERT
LOVE IN THE SIXTIES

In my youth I relished the thought that when I retired, I would have
all the time there is. That would be true about my freedom to choose
what to do each day; but of course when I did retire I was very aware that
I had fewer days remaining to enjoy that freedom. I intended to make
the best of them.

In 1998 as we were nearing retirement, my wife Zhita persuaded me
to join her in an aerobics class at a YMCA. Before long we were going to
a fitness center, and I was doing my first regular exercise in more than
40 years (since Navy boot camp). As I found that I felt better and came
to appreciate the benefits of exercise, I started paying more attention to
my health. I shed 40 of my 200 pounds in a couple of years, and I walked
with a new spring in my step. Retirement might last a little longer.

After we settled down in retirement, art classes provided my main activity. I had never taken an art class before, but in 2000 I went to Santa Monica College to begin learning about design, drawing, sculpture, ceramics and glassblowing. While enrolled in just two or three classes each semester, I was in effect a fulltime student.

Late in 2001 I saw a poster for an outdoor club enticing me to join and train for a hike in the Grand Canyon from the North Rim to the South Rim. I signed up. Many years before I had hiked in that canyon several times, but I had never tried it rim to rim. The dumbest hike I ever took was in the canyon, in the summer before my senior year in high school in 1952. I was working as a soda jerk at the Bright Angel Lodge, and several of us with summer jobs at the canyon wanted to see what it was like down at the bottom. We all had only one day off each week, and someone thought of hiking down after work on a night with a full moon. We could sleep a while at the bottom, get meals at Phantom Ranch and then hike back out. To accommodate all our work schedules, we met at midnight one night at the head of the steep South Kaibab Trail, clad in ordinary clothes including shoes with smooth leather soles. My supplies for the hike consisted of a quart canteen of water and a pack of cigarettes.

Somehow we made it to Phantom Ranch at about 4:00 am, and we stretched out to sleep on wooden benches we found around the swimming pool they had then. We got up to eat breakfast at the ranch and then went out sightseeing. We returned for lunch, and each of us also bought a boxed lunch to go. After filling our quart canteens, we started up the Bright Angel Trail to return to the rim. Indian Gardens offered the only source of water along the nine mile trail in those days, and there was no source of food. We climbed 4,500 ft. to reach the top at about 2:00 am, so hungry and thirsty that I would have cheerfully paid a week's wages for a hamburger and a milkshake. No restaurants or markets were open in the village. Getting out of bed some hours later to go back to work after too little sleep was almost more than I could do. I did not want to repeat an experience like that.

In the late 1960's and early 70's, a few years older and a little wiser, I went with some friends on occasional hikes. A couple of times we simply hiked down into that canyon, hiked out, and then hurt for a week. That was what hiking was like, in my experience, enjoyable but not a compelling recreation. I had never heard of training for a hike until that outdoor club poster caught my attention.

Training for a hike is a good idea. Like workouts in a gym, practice hikes while carrying gradually increasing backpack loads serve to strengthen muscles, and hiking prepares muscles for challenges which are quite different from routine walking. Carrying the pack weight for extended distances on uneven surfaces uphill and especially downhill was an ideal way to prepare my muscles for the work and also my heart and lungs for delivering oxygen to my muscles. Wearing hiking boots while training also seemed to help condition my feet to the boots.

To my surprise, while training with the club I discovered that my old knees didn't do so well hiking downhill with a loaded pack. I was glad I did not first discover this on my way into the depths of the Grand Canyon. Was it too late for me to begin backpacking again? But I *really* wanted to do this.

The club leader recommended that I get a pair of trekking poles to reduce the impact on my knees while going downhill with a pack. I found that learning to use the poles to reduce the impact and also continuing to strengthen my leg muscles with more training solved that problem for me. The pain disappeared, and my knees felt secure once again. It turned out that another benefit of using poles was that they helped me to keep my balance when loose gravel or soil moved under my feet, so using the poles was well worth the trouble.

On a training hike in the San Jacinto Mountains near Palm Springs I realized that higher altitude, even just 7,000 or 8,000 ft., was more challenging for me than for others in the club. I lagged behind the younger hikers going uphill at that altitude more than I did at lower elevations. I had to stop to catch my breath more often. Perhaps the old scar tissue in my lungs reduced my lung capacity more than the 10% my doctor had estimated. I had been surprised when the scar was discovered in an x-ray taken to verify that a mild case of pneumonia was cleared up, and I speculated that I had been exposed to asbestos years before when I was working on ships. Now concerned about hiking in thin air, I asked my doctor if it was safe. Assured that the scar tissue would not be provoked into some unwelcome activity, I decided to continue. There was no pain and no real danger, I was simply challenged to get enough oxygen. I could hike at altitude, just a little more slowly. I determined to keep on hiking, taking time as needed to acclimate.

Backpack design and construction in 2001 were surprisingly different from what I remembered, with internal frames and lighter materials - and that was just the beginning. Boots and water containers were much improved as well. My old hiking boots each weighed about two pounds more than modern boots. I had a lot to learn about modern equipment, and I avidly read about backpacking gear and practices and quizzed the staff at outdoor equipment stores.

After several months the training was over, and in 2002 we began our descent from the North Rim. The other hikers in the club shared my concern about whether I, the 66 year old, would be able to hike back up to the 7,000 ft. South Rim of the canyon. Several offered to help carry my equipment on the way out. Two days later I actually completed the rim to rim hike, without any help. At the top I called Zhita and exclaimed that the hike was wonderful! I was triumphant. I felt like turning around and hiking right back down into the canyon and up the other side. On the way home I proudly wore my new tee shirt emblazoned with my cartoon of hikers clambering up out of the canyon.

Exultant, I envisioned my next hiking adventure. I began by persuading my daughters Darbi and Kirsten, my brother John, my brother-in-law Neil and several friends to repeat the Grand Canyon hike with me the following year. Training for the hike had made a big difference for me, so I preached training and exercise to our group. Training regimens were not equal for each of us, but in 2003 everyone made it to the top. I loved it. Driving home to Los Angeles after that hike I gazed at mountains ranging for miles alongside the highway and thought "I want to hike and be *going somewhere!*" Hiking had turned out to be great fun as well as good exercise, but hiking far more than 24 miles through a canyon could be a true adventure.

When I first told my daughters about intending to hike through the Grand Canyon at my advanced age, Kirsten had sent me a copy of Bill Bryson's book, ***A Walk in the Woods***. It was hilarious, and I now found it had planted a seed in my own thoughts. Hiking a long trail like the Appalachian Trail was conceivable, even for the inexperienced and even for the no longer young. It seemed like a wonderful adventure. I had heard about the Pacific Crest Trail in the western US, and that became the focus of my new desire to hike and be going somewhere. If Bryson could tackle the AT, I could try the PCT.

My father had worked for the U.S. Forest Service his whole career, so I grew up with outdoor recreation as part of life. When I was old enough Dad took me hunting and fishing for several days each year. I learned to pay attention in the woods, to notice my surroundings and the movements of wild life. I had to try to develop a sense of where I was in order to reach a destination and also to keep track of how to find my way back to our car. Often we were on no trail. Whenever Dad left me alone for a while, say when I looked for deer on one ridge and he walked away to check out another, I was very conscious of the risk of getting lost. Dad also made sure I was conscious of the risk of shooting without being certain that a legal buck was my target.

I asked Dad how he could spot game animals when it was so hard for me to see them. He taught me to look for such things as a horizontal line among the vertical lines of tree trunks and a spot with a contrasting shade of gray or brown. The back of a deer may stand out as a horizontal line among trees, and a deer's color is likely to appear slightly different from that of its surroundings. I learned the value of noticing what looked a little unusual or out of place – once something caught my eye, I could study it in order to determine what I was looking at.

Now having lived in sprawling Los Angeles for thirty years, I had not spent much recreation time outside of cities. I had not thought about what I learned so long ago in the outdoors. Still, it seemed natural that in hiking the PCT I would live outdoors for extended periods of time and that I might hike much of the trail alone. I had rarely ever camped alone in the woods, but I supposed that many hikers did it routinely on the PCT.

I announced to Zhita that I had decided to hike the incredibly long trail from Mexico to Canada, more than 2,650 miles (4,280 km). I wanted to hike the whole trail at once because I wasn't sure I could still be hiking for many more years. (I had not seen any seniors getting around with walkers or wheelchairs which were rated for off-road use in the mountains.) Zhita was unmoved by this rationale. After much further discussion ("We're still married, aren't we?"), I agreed to be a bit sensible and hike just a piece of the trail at a time. Guesstimating how long the hike would take me and how many more years I might enjoy hiking, I settled on approximately 400 mile sections (640 km) each summer for seven years. That should take me away from home for only five weeks or so at a time instead of five months. Zhita was much more comfortable with that prospect. This compromise came with a risk, I knew, for at my age I might discover I did not have that many years left to enjoy hiking. Still, the prospect of such an adventure was exciting. I would do it.

Zhita observed my new enthusiasm with quiet amusement. She had seen me through my excitement about earlier projects, such as when I decided to learn about model railroads so I could build a train layout modeled after the careers of each of my grandfathers. Over four or five years I had joined the National Model Railroad Association, the Railroad and Locomotive Historical Society and several local model railroad groups. I went to model railroad and historical railroad conferences, read books, journals and catalogs, and took hundreds of photos of old trains and related buildings and equipment. I learned about the Kansas City Southern trains and equipment my maternal grandfather had worked on in Oklahoma in the early 1900's and that of the Pennsylvania

Railroad my paternal grandfather had worked on in Pennsylvania. My enthusiasm was gradually sidetracked when I became engrossed in taking art classes. I felt sure the project was just postponed for a while.

Another major project had been making an upside down aquarium. While I was involved with creating sculptures in an art class, I decided I wanted to make a new kind of aquarium. I enjoyed seeing aquariums with beautiful fish and appropriate scenery, but the container holding the water and fish was not interesting. Why not make the aquarium itself a sculpture, so I could enjoy both the aquarium and the aquatic scene inside? I envisioned a sculpted figure rising gracefully from a shallow tray of water, boldly poised, perhaps precariously, with the surprising feature of fish swimming leisurely inside. (Years later it struck me that I wanted to view the aquarium itself somewhat as the artist James Turrell promotes viewing light itself, aside from what it illuminates.)

It turned out to be complicated to make an inverted aquarium in which fish could actually live towering above a shallow tray. That might explain why I had not seen any. Making a suitable sculpture was only one of the challenges. I found that I could pump the air out of an experimental inverted aquarium I placed in a tray filled with water, and with care I could keep adding water to the tray as the resulting vacuum lifted water to fill the inverted aquarium. To keep fish alive inside, I needed to aerate the water in the aquarium to replenish the oxygen without admitting air bubbles, because, of course, air would release the vacuum holding the water up inside the inverted container. The fish needed to be fed in there, and somehow the aquarium must be cleaned regularly. Introducing light and color into the sculpture to complement the moving fish in the water within was a feature I was still just imagining. Living in earthquake country as I do, I also would need to secure the heavy, towering inverted container so that a shake would not topple it, releasing gallons of water and gravely inconveniencing the fish, not to mention my wife.

The aquarium project had to be interrupted because now I wanted to take a series of extended hikes, requiring a lot of time for planning, preparing, training and especially being away while hiking. The fish in my experimental aquarium would not survive my extended inattention, so I returned my fish to the pet shop and set aside my tanks and pumps and apparatus. I would find that art classes also interfered with hiking preparations, so the following fall I would discontinue the classes. My model train gear remained on the sidelines, as I turned my full attention to my new challenge, the hike.

I sent out an email to entice my Grand Canyon hiking partners and a few other friends to join me in hiking the PCT, at least for sections of it. The quickest, most enthusiastic response came from Kirsten, my younger daughter, who was already thinking about such an adventure and the possibility of recruiting someone to hike with her. Unfortunately, the reality of limited free time while keeping her job would prevent her from major participation for now. My older daughter, Darbi, also responded warmly to the idea, but she too had limited time available away from her work.

I described the opportunity in glowing terms to my recently retired brother, John, who had become a hiking enthusiast because of the 2003 Grand Canyon hike. He was definitely intrigued. Later, after receiving and studying my hike plan, John decided to hike with me for the first three weeks. That would take him 145 miles on the PCT (his first long hike as well). "I'll hike with you to try to find out why you're doing this," he said, making it clear that my attempts at explaining the allure of this adventure were not entirely persuasive. His friend Jennie, another new hiking enthusiast, said she would hike with us for the last week of John's hike (about 35 miles, her longest hike at the time). Zhita and I were both reassured to know that I would begin hiking the unfamiliar trail with someone I knew.

My friend Gene, who was semiretired, decided to do a day hike with me in each year he could arrange to do it while I was hiking the PCT. He knew that joining me on such a long hike would require a lot of traveling to and from the portions of the trail he would walk with me, and he was willing to do that in order to share this adventure. Some of my other friends were interested in participating, too, so I kept them on my email list for updates about my plans. Shared experiences hiking together promised to enrich my hiking experiences as well as my relationships with family members and with friends. Solo hiking remained my prospect for most miles of the trail, and that would turn out to be a prized part of my experience.

I read that a popular time to begin hiking the PCT from the Mexican border is the last weekend in April. That usually allows time for the previous winter's snow to melt enough to allow hikers to get through the nearby San Jacinto Mountains in southern California, while usually allowing faster hikers to reach the Canadian border before fall's new snow gets too deep. Accordingly, the Annual Day Zero Pacific Crest Trail Kick Off (ADZPCTKO) gathering was held near the southern end of the trail during that April weekend. I decided to time the beginning of my hike so I could join that gathering. The Kick Off presented a good opportunity to meet with other hikers and to learn about current trail conditions in southern California.

I didn't know anyone who had hiked a long trail, but I read a lot about it and began intense planning, training and preparing. I replaced my synthetic fill sleeping bag from the Grand Canyon hikes with a much lighter bag filled with down, and I replaced things like my vintage Primus stove which was hard to light in cold weather. I began reading about food and nutrition for hikers. I get skin cancer, so there was no question that I would always hike in long sleeves and pants and a wide-brimmed hat, in addition to using sunscreen. One of my skin cancers had been a melanoma, and one was enough.

To compensate for my lack of experience, I decided to make a spreadsheet detailing how many miles I would hike each day, noting elevation gains and losses to be faced and where I was likely to sleep each night for the first 450 miles. To track my progress, I also included each day's final mileage from the starting point at the Mexican border. Such a hike plan was made possible by the detailed information in the PCT guidebook, Pacific Crest Trail Southern California, and in the

Pacific Crest Trail Data Book. I did not meet anyone else who made such detailed plans, but my hike plan turned out to be very helpful for me.

Taking suggestions I gleaned from a backpacking manual, I also plotted when and where I could access a road to resupply approximately weekly, so I didn't have to carry too much food at one time. I had read that this was standard practice among long distance hikers. For my first year's hike on the trail, I planned to resupply either by meeting Zhita and retrieving my resupply bag holding the food I had prepared for the following week or by hitching a ride to a nearby town to buy what I needed. For this year I did not plan to try an alternative practice of mailing packages of supplies to myself in care of General Delivery. I also devised a checklist of which items to place where in my backpack, another spreadsheet I would revise from experience each year. I learned a lot in the process of planning and preparing for my hike for the first section of the trail, but once on the trail I would find that I still had a lot to learn – no surprise.

Included in my training for my first PCT hike was another Grand Canyon hike in early April of 2004, this time down the South Kaibab Trail to the river and then back up the Bright Angel Trail, all on the South Rim. This was bad timing so near the PCT hike, but snow and ice on the canyon rim prevented us from doing it earlier in the year. I hiked with John, Neil and a wonderful group of friends. This somewhat less ambitious hike in the Grand Canyon still seemed challenging but now almost routine, just a strenuous part of my training for the PCT. On our way out of the canyon Neil grimly announced, "I'll never do anything so stupid as to hike into that canyon again," making it clear that my more intensive training was worth the effort.

However, the Grand Canyon hike in the midst of my art classes consumed much precious time. I needed to provide a more realistic amount of time for getting ready for my PCT hike. Now I had to scramble to complete the many final details of my preparations.

Zhita's Story

Probably most people who know me would agree that I am a responsible person. Most people really respect that, and I enjoy and value their respect. But, for me, responsibility is also The Big R—hanging over my head always, and moving me in directions that I deem responsible. In every school, from kindergarten through high school, I was the reliable kid. Teachers loved it, and I was proud to be doing the right thing. But responsibility also comes with built-in mandates—you have to do, always. And that is not always welcome.

I grew up in New York City during the period of what we now call The Great Depression, a period followed by World War II. Our family would probably have been classified as lower middle class. My father had a variety of jobs—a "checker" in restaurants who stood by the kitchen door to check the outgoing trays of food to be sure that they were as ordered—before starting his own business as a "printing broker." He sought commercial clients who needed printed advertisements and other communications and he worked with them to provide the kinds of materials that would meet those needs. He didn't have a printing press, just a desk in someone else's office from which he could make his phone calls and make all the connections necessary to deliver the product that the customer wanted. He might write or edit the text himself, then connect with commercial artists who could do the art work and design, before taking the original to one of many commercial printers to make the copies. Assembly of materials was accomplished in a variety of ways. Sometimes he even brought the materials home, laid them out on a table, and consulted with us for potential ideas. As he explained to us, he was selling his services, not just a product. To my amazement, he had some pretty big commercial clients with names that even I recognized. And this is how he supported our family, bought a house, sent two of us to college, etc....

My mom was a very dedicated and responsible partner who knew how to use money wisely and even how to support my father in his business efforts. It was she who kept the financial records; she was a de facto secretary and bookkeeper who worked at home—in addition to being a very devoted mother. She was very health conscious and wanted to make sure that we ate well—even on a small budget and with food stamp rationing. She took nutrition classes and planned the healthiest menus, then shopped all over town—without a car, of course—to find the healthiest food. The plates were always heaped with food that was colorfully balanced (a way to ensure good nutrition) and very tasty. My father always referred to her as "a good plain cook," a phrase that I would aggressively take him to task for if he were here today. But he adored my mom and ate every bit of food on his plate.

My father was also very determined that we be our own persons--"If you are doing the right thing, don't worry about what other people think." And that we be independent. That goal of independence also determined the way he taught us to travel.

As renters in New York City, we lived in many different neighborhoods—the Bronx, Queens, Nassau ...and we had many relatives who lived in various parts of the city. Like most New Yorkers at that time, we had no car, and we relied on the system of subways and buses to get us wherever we needed to go. When we were quite young, my parents taught us how to navigate the system on our own. My brother Howard, three years younger, and I would walk a mile to the bus, ride to the subway, then on to our destination. We loved to get in the first car of the train and stand looking out on the tracks as we whizzed from station to station. We learned to read the subway maps, noting which car line stopped where, express and local stops, and transfer points. My parents and we seemed very comfortable with our getting around this way—even though I realize in retrospect that I do not remember any other kids I knew doing this. And I would have to say that navigating this system, even at age 9 or 10, was a lot easier than trying to find my dear one on the PCT. But I guess this was good preparation for proceeding without fear, confident that Jim and I would eventually find the right meeting place. Little did I know the challenges....

Reflecting on what enabled me to take on my role as my Dear One's support person, it strikes me that I had a remarkable role model. Isn't that what my Mom did—always! It was her idea that my dad start his own business, and, when he did, she became the at-home bookkeeper. There was also a remarkable period when my parents decided that Dad, who always got sick in the winter, had rheumatic fever, etc., should go to Florida for a few months in the winter to see if that climate would make a difference in his health. While he was gone, my mother actually ran the business, went to the office in Manhattan and kept things going at the office and at home. As I reflect on that now, it was amazing—but that's what a wife and mother did—provided support to husband and family in any way that was needed.

I think about my style of relating to people and also my comfort in being alone. I enjoy all kinds of people; I am not shy and feel comfortable in approaching anyone to ask questions, make comments, just connect. If I have a question I never hesitate to ask whoever might help. I have an inherent respect for all people—inherent probably but also consciously taught by my parents. "No one is beneath you; treat people with the same respect you would like from others." How often that need to question played out on the PCT. Ask everyone, anyone, the same question many times just to make sure that you're on the right track—or, more accurately, the right trail. The only problem I was not prepared for was that often there was no one around to ask.

That ability to relate to and feel comfortable with all people was also extended through the absolutely unanticipated—unthinkable!—life that I stumbled into as a young adult. As a graduate student at the University of Wisconsin, I met Ralph, a handsome, charming man who, unthinkably, became my first husband. Ralph was an African American man who lived in Madison, Wisconsin, and hung around the university as a social activity. When one of my dorm mates in graduate school invited a group of us to go out for ice cream with some guys from town, it sounded like fun. Ralph was charming, remarkably handsome, and quite interested in me. The rest is a very important part of my history.

As Ralph and I dated, I realized that Madison, Wisconsin, was not the right place for a black guy to lead a decent life. I urged Ralph to leave and find a better place—any place—to make his future. He listened to my persuasive argument and chose Los Angeles. He left and I continued graduate school, and that should have been the end of that story. But it wasn't…. Ralph loved LA, called to say that I must come to see him, and I did…. I never left.

Ralph and I married, eventually had two daughters, and lived a good life together for about 14 years. During that time, I became an intimately connected member of the African American community. While LA was a very integrated city and open in many ways, I soon became aware of the issues which are inherent in our society and which affect African Americans at every moment of every day. For many reasons, Ralph and I were not suitable partners. Especially as we grew older, the differences in our education (Ralph had never finished high school), and our maturing styles affected our relationship and our family. Ralph and I divorced but have remained friends throughout the years.

Why do I add this chapter in my life? Because moving into black culture in America is like moving into a different world—or, perhaps more accurate—moving in the same world with new eyes, with a new mind. How were my new people, my new family perceived? How was I perceived in this new world? How should I navigate—figuratively, if not literally? I learned so much about the plight of being Black in America. As a Jew, I understood about anti-Semitism, but I did not feel affected by it. I was proud to be among the "chosen people." I soon realized in ways that I could never have understood that African Americans did not feel and were not perceived as "chosen." Navigating a new culture surely prepared me in unique ways for living anywhere along the PCT route and making it on my own.

And, of course, besides the cultural differences of my new people, I was living in LA, a very different city from New York. Subways? There were none. City? Where was it? A few tall buildings in a vastly spread-out landscape of what we used to call "bungalows." Where were the museums, the theaters, the people??? I would search and find the things that interested me. And, when I did, I was developing a new skill that has enabled me to find something of interest wherever I happen to be.

Another factor in my life that may have helped with trail-tracking my husband was the career path that I both followed and forged. I started my career as an elementary school teacher because I needed to help support my family and that was the career path available to women in those years. But, with classrooms of 35-40 wiggly 3rd, 4th, or 5th graders, I was not a very effective teacher. I was interested in concepts and in talking through issues; the little guys were not impressed. But I got lucky. In the mid-60s, the federal Elementary and Secondary Education Act provided funds for special projects in what were then called Title I schools. These were schools where poverty and low levels of academic achievement were handicapping whole communities. As part of the Los Angeles Unified School District (LAUSD) Title I program, they funded an experimental project. They identified 10 teachers who would become "teacher librarians," a new position open to teachers who would serve all students in the targeted schools using the previously unstaffed school library as a classroom. The goal was to get kids to read and to enjoy reading. There was no program so we had to design our own. Each of us was assigned to two or three schools. Wow! What a joy! I loved it. I browsed the library shelves, found books I wanted to share with kids and then thought about what kinds of related information I could teach them—about the library, about research, about the subjects of the books...

What a difference that made in my teaching and in my life! Now kids were spellbound rather than wiggly—and I was thinking of creative ways to teach them what I now realize are research skills. I went on from there to coordinate that program for LAUSD and to train teachers and teacher librarians to think more creatively about research, literature (something about which I was passionate and for which I had a Master's degree) and problem solving. I wrote pioneering professional books about something that I dubbed Information Literacy, and I had such a good time. I had found my professional niche. I believe my information literacy skills helped to guide me in my searches for my husband: How should I think about this? What is the most likely place to get information? What should I be looking for at the trail site?

My personal learning and working style were also helpful. Early on in my professional life in LA, I realized that I have an inclination for collaboration. In my professional roles where I was providing leadership and coordination for staff at school, district and county levels, I learned that, although I had grown up in a culture where you were taught to do things on your own, I had both inclination and skills for effective collaboration. Working with others to achieve common goals was very important to me. It gave me pleasure and feelings of satisfaction and accomplishment. Helping other people fulfill their goals was a delight. Helping my beloved achieve his goal was a privilege; it was more than worth the challenge!

2004 Innocence

Ignorance more frequently begets
confidence than does knowledge...

CHARLES DARWIN
THE DESCENT OF MAN

But without such ignorance...how could we live?

MARGARET ATWOOD
THE BLIND ASSASSIN

My two successful Grand Canyon hikes seemed like a reasonable apprenticeship for a major hike, and with all my planning, preparing and training I felt well prepared for my first attempt at hiking a long distance. My confidence would be put to the test. Looking back, Zhita called this the year of innocence – or as I say, ignorance.

On Wednesday, April 21, John drove from his home in Phoenix to Kamp Anza Kampgroud near the small town of Anza, CA where Zhita and I would meet him. The plan was for him to leave his truck there and ride with us to Campo, near the US border with Mexico. He would complete his hike with me near Anza and then retrieve his truck for the drive home. John and I would begin hiking from the border to reach Lake Morena in time for the ADZPCTKO weekend gathering where we hoped to learn more about hiking this trail. But at my home I was still frantically printing maps with new software on the day we were to meet John, so Zhita and I didn't pick him up in Anza until late in the afternoon. We arrived at our motel near Campo after dark. Early next morning we enjoyed a hearty breakfast at the nearby casino before driving to the trailhead at the Mexican border.

When we arrived at the trailhead, I was shocked to discover that I had forgotten my boots in the last-minute rush. Zhita sensibly urged that we go home for the boots and return the next day to begin the hike. But I didn't want to miss a day of the ADZPCTKO event. I was ready, eager to go. I decided to set out wearing what I had worn in the car, my Birkenstock sandals, even though I had never trained for hiking in sandals. My sandals offered no ankle support, limited foot protection and worn, shallow grooves in the soles for traction – reminiscent of my footwear for my boyhood hike into the Grand Canyon.

Zhita

For months, Jim has been studying and preparing for the start of the great PCT Adventure. Today is the day it begins… hopefully. I am dressed and ready to drive him and his brother John southeast to the deserted edge of California where the two of them plan to start their hike tomorrow morning. We need to leave so that we can reach John on time; but Jim is glued to the computer in a mode of determination and frenzy. He is printing—or trying to print—the maps that he will need to follow the trail.

Recognizing his silent frenzy—and my uselessness—I sit downstairs and try to read. I am very aware of the clock; the minutes, then hours are ticking away; we have a few hours' drive to meet John at a roadside where he will leave his car after driving from Phoenix. I watch the clock…. And watch the clock…. And wait for the sound of Jim's footsteps on the stairs. There is nothing I can do or say; the stress continues…. And then, finally, he appears. The look on his face is not reassuring.

When he lifts his pack to take it to the car, I am stunned to see how heavy it is. How can he possibly walk with that pack? But the adventure is about to begin and we must be on our way. It is good to be moving.... After a couple of hours, we meet up with John and go out to eat. For me, eating is always a wonderful respite—relax and enjoy... We drive on to the motel in which we plan to spend the night. But it is getting dark, and the road is unfamiliar. Are we going the right way? Can we make it? More stress.... What a relief when we finally arrive after dark to settle in for the night.

The next morning begins cheerfully. We are on our way to the border; the hike will begin; and everyone is in good spirits. I am very happy to see the adventure beginning. Jim and John each check their packs, then change from sandals to their boots.... or not. Jim has just discovered that he has left his boots at home!! I am stunned—and so sad for him; of course, we will drive back to LA to get the boots and make another start.... But that's my vision, not Jim's.

He is determined to start immediately—with a huge pack and Birkenstock sandals!!! And, he tells me, with a smile, that I, Zhita, will drive back to LA, get the boots and return in two days to meet them at the PCT Kick-Off Party. He can't be serious! But he is.... What chutzpah! That's my immediate reaction. But I love him dearly and treasure our partnership so I head for LA with lots of time to muse about the dramatic start of this grand adventure. And, when I do return to meet the guys at the Kickoff Party, I participate in the party atmosphere, meet some of the other hikers, and leave reassured that Jim will be appropriately shod and travelling with good people. I realize in retrospect that this was my inauguration to the great adventure.

Jim

John and I posed for Zhita to take our picture at the trail marker at the Mexican border, the beginning of the trail. I pushed my toes under the fence along the border so I could say I really started out from Mexico.

Then she watched as John and I began our trek. An inauspicious beginning, but the hike was on.

The trail led us through chaparral, initially consisting of thick sagebrush with a sprinkling of cactus. As we climbed up on a high ridge, we
felt weighed down. We started out with over 55 lb. packs, but we soon decided that five liters of water was enough for each of us to carry. Pouring
out the other four liters helped. Hiking in the desert with temperatures
in the 90's wasn't all that bad, and we had less than 20 miles to go to the
first water supply. Several clusters of faster hikers passed us during the
day and even in the dark after we were in our tents.

I learned to automatically wiggle my feet to shake out sand and gravel when it got into my sandals, and I was pretty careful to avoid kicking
things, especially cactus.   Hiking those miles in sandals turned out
to be somewhat clumsy for me but manageable. Still, I did not want
to continue without boots any longer than I had to. We reached Lake
Morena, site of the ADZPCTKO gathering, on Friday morning without
mishap, convinced by then that somehow reducing our pack weight was
important.

It was great to meet so many young and experienced hikers, so full
of enthusiasm. Two or three hundred of them were setting out to "thru
hike" the entire trail in one long summer. I enjoyed hearing stories of
their various backgrounds, preparations and expectations for this hike.
I was 68 years old then, and I saw that, while not the oldest hiker at the
Kick Off, my white beard showed that I was older than the fathers of
many of those hikers. In the evening a gray haired hiker in a nearby
campsite called out to me that he and I were probably the only hikers in
the campground who were flossing their teeth on the trail.

Some of the hikers used trail names, nicknames adopted or be-
stowed on them as hiking monikers. Names like Mad Monte Dodge
or Meadow Ed were descriptive of some trait. A man camped next to
us introduced himself as Grandad, a name he had chosen when he was
hiking the Appalachian Trail. John proposed that my trail name should
be "Shoeless Jim," after my mishap at the beginning of our hike. That

would have been a good name for me, but I had not seen the movie and so I did not know what connotations the name might carry. Not knowing how I might come to view such a trail name in the future, I declined to use it - a choice I later saw as timid.

The most valuable information we received at the meeting was about the current year's water availability, which streams and springs described in the trail guide were actually wet at that time and which were dry. Meadow Ed and a few other volunteers had scouted them out just before the Kick Off. We also learned about occasional water caches maintained by wonderful "trail angels" - volunteers who helped hikers by doing such things as stashing gallon bottles of water on some dry stretches of the trail. A few angels maintained multiple caches. We were cautioned to regard caches as a bonus and not to depend on finding water there when we arrived, though in longer dry stretches we actually needed to rely on caches. Trail angels were usually sometime hikers themselves or else family or friends of hikers. They understood how much it could mean for a hiker to find a cache in a dry stretch of trail. Sometimes a cache near a road was stocked with a cooler filled with sodas and sport drinks.

We also learned more about lightening pack loads, and John and I each set aside some unnecessary equipment to send home with Zhita – which would relieve her as much as it did us. For example, John reduced his 8 or 9 cooking/eating utensils to 4 (later to just a pot and a "spork," a spoon with stubby prongs), socks and underwear for 5 days cut to 2 (we decided to rinse out socks and briefs along the way), shirts 5 to 2, pants 2 to 1, 3 water containers reduced to 2. John also eliminated "comforts" such as his razor, shaving cream, after-shave, and an extra book which no longer seemed important to carry.

The next day Zhita arrived at Lake Morena with my boots and a picnic feast. What a welcome sight she was! She was very glad to see that we were none the worse for our first small trek through a desert portion of the trail. My feet and ankles had survived the sandal test. We introduced her to some of our new friends in the campground and then we shared with a couple of them the extravagant feast she had brought for lunch.

Smiling once again, she took our excess gear and my Birkenstocks and headed for home.

As the Kick Off drew to a close, John and I loaded our packs and made our way north. The trail ahead was a sampler of terrains to hike through on our trek toward Canada. We would leave behind the desert chaparral and cactus as we climbed into the Laguna Mountains which I envisioned clad in a forest of Jeffrey Pine and black oak at an altitude of 6,000 ft. We would descend again into desert landscape and then begin the long ascent into the San Jacinto Mountains, where the trail attains 9,000 ft. along the crest. Hiking solo by then, I would descend into the desert once more before climbing Mt. San Gorgonio and on into the forested San Gabriel Mountains.

After hiking up into the Lagunas John and I had a hard time suppressing our laughter while we watched a young man struggling in the wind with his mylar-covered umbrella (advocated by Ray Jardine, early guru of ultralight backpacking). Carrying the reflective umbrella was supposed to make it unnecessary to carry a poncho or rain suit, a hat and a signal mirror for emergencies. This hiker righted his umbrella repeatedly when the wind turned it inside out, until finally the poor guy plunged the umbrella into a convenient campground trash can in exasperation. It was a memorable scene.

Soon we met up with the venerable Billy Goat, a legend of the PCT. He was a lanky 65 years old then, with long gray hair and beard, and he had spent most of his life hiking since he retired at age 55. He had hiked all of the PCT a number of times, and he had also hiked the Appalachian Trail, the Continental Divide Trail (thus earning the Triple Crown) and many other trails. We found him talking to a few other hikers, and we stopped to join them. As we stood talking about the trail conditions and water sources, Billy Goat poured some water into a cup and added some grain. When I asked about his snack food, he explained that he was eating muesli because of his diabetes. He said that when he wanted to make something special of his meal, he heated the water. He was carrying only muesli to eat, but his diet was varied whenever he met up with his wife Mary, who was driving their motor home along roads near the trail. She was also a blessed trail angel, stopping at times where she could reach the trail to offer hikers an ice chest filled with cold drinks.

I had planned an easy pace for our first week on the trail, 60 miles in 5 days. Consequently, John and I arrived early at Scissors Crossing at Highway 78. Zhita and our friend Ann arrived at noon, as planned. It was wonderful to see them. Zhita was amused to hear that John was still trying to find an answer to his question about why I was doing this hike.

Zhita: First Meet-up

It's time to meet Jim and John for their first respite from the trail. Since the meeting will be near the charming town of Julian, one of our favorite places to wander, my dear friend Ann decides to join me so we can visit and do a little exploring. We arrange for two motel rooms—one for Ann and me and one for Jim and John. (This is certainly not the way I would plan in the future; ideally, I would, of course, be with my beloved.)

When the guys call, I drive out to meet them at the road where they have left the trail. There they sit, dirty and weary and definitely ready for a respite. It is clear that Jim is greatly stressed, but his hugs are warm and wonderful as always. The guys retreat to their room, remove their filthy clothes and give them to me to revive them. I check around for the local laundry and find that the nearest one is in Ramona, 20 plus miles away. I sigh and head on out. Jim is so exhausted that my food-loving guy chooses to eat lunch and dinner in the same restaurant! Fatigue conquers all desire for further adventure—even dining choices.

The following day, we drive the guys back to the trail, then Ann and I go back to LA. I am more relaxed today, but there is a sense of personal loss without Jim.

Jim

On our second day after Julian, John noticed poison oak flourishing in shady gullies along the trail. It was much more pervasive here than we had seen previously along the trail, and we took care to avoid brushing against it. Neither of us had had contact with poison oak or ivy in many years, but I well remembered my maddening blisters from contacting poison ivy as a kid. We were fortunate to avoid any allergic reaction to the poison oak this time. I studied the triple leaves of the noxious plant, knowing I would need to be more alert to its appearance when I was hiking alone.

Trail angels brightened several of our days with water caches in this semi-arid land. We appreciated the ready-to-use water, in spite of the clutter it makes beside the trail. Later that day we filtered more water and bathed a bit at a scum and algae covered stock tank about a half mile from where we had set up camp beside dry San Felipe Creek. Next morning clear water was flowing in the creek, with no sign of a storm anywhere. Where had the water come from? That was one of many puzzles along the way. We stopped to take pictures at Eagle Rock, as most everyone does. The natural rock formation looks remarkably like an eagle standing nearly twenty feel tall just off the trail.

Having hiked for more miles than I ever had before, I was having a major problem with blisters on my feet. By the time we reached Warner Springs, where John's friend Jennie came to meet us so she could hike with us for a week, I had a lot of blisters. John had few. I bandaged my blisters as well as I could, but walking on them made me grit my teeth. I was determined to keep hiking and to keep on schedule, especially since Zhita as well as John and Jennie had made their plans to fit mine. John and I had hiked 110 miles so far, much of it in hot weather. When Jennie saw the blisters covering the balls of my feet and my heels, she suddenly wasn't so sure about hiking with us.

I learned only slowly that I needed to remove my boots and socks every hour or two while hiking in hot weather, so my sweaty feet could cool and dry a bit. (John and many other hikers don't need to do this, but for me that's what worked.) The combination of heat and moisture with the friction between feet and boots readily gave me blisters. In cooler weather I would find that I could hike three hours or more before removing my boots.

Over the Hill

We talked with Jennie about the hike before us, gradually climbing above the desert, and she made up her mind that she would hike with us after all. Her son Joe, who had driven her from Phoenix to our meeting place near Warner Springs, took our picture and very reluctantly said goodbye. Joe really hated to leave his mom with two scruffy guys out in the middle of nowhere, especially after seeing my blisters.

As the trail took us up toward Mt. San Jacinto through higher desert chaparral country, I had my most memorable small wildlife encounter. We could look down to our right from this arid mountain ridge and see Borrego Springs Desert State Park. We were actually within the park boundaries on that ridge. The weather was very hot and dry, and the trail took us through a devastating burn that had left little more than tall charcoal skeletons of bushes standing in a deep layer of gray ash blanketing the ground. The chaparral in this area had included chamise, also known as greasewood, which burns very hot. Signs of life returning to this desolate country were limited to occasional patches of grasses and small flowers, no more than six or eight inches tall. The oppressive heat persuaded us to take a midafternoon break. At Jennie's suggestion, we took a couple of tent ground cloths from our packs and tied them to the charred sticks to get some shade. Then I needed to pee.

I walked back down the trail around a ridge for some privacy. There was no place to hide in this stark landscape, so I just stood on the edge of the trail. As I was standing there, I heard a familiar sound. Looking down, I saw a bright green hummingbird which flew between my legs, paused in midair to get a quick drink, and then flew on! I was astonished. Hot, dry, desolate landscape indeed! Compared with the plight of that hummingbird, my hiking in the heat while carrying a supply of water and food seemed not such a bad fate after all. Through the years on the PCT I encountered rattlesnakes, a bobcat, a fox, marmots, pikas and other small critters, plus deer, elk, bear and many birds. But I think I'll never forget sharing a rest break with that little hummingbird.

Soon after we started hiking again, we walked along the base of scorched Horsesnort Mountain, rising on our left. At times I joked with

John and Jennie that some stretches of the trail seemed designed by someone who thought he would be paid by the mile (winding the trail around mountain ridges a lot rather than climbing or descending a little), while other stretches of the trail seemed plotted to earn someone a bonus by taking the shortest possible route (climbing or descending steeply rather than winding around or constructing switchbacks).

John had discovered on his earlier Grand Canyon hikes that he loved to eat "gorp" as a snack food, so he had packed some for each day on this PCT hike. Eating "good old raisins and peanuts" (and M&M's) every day had an unforeseen and unfortunate consequence: he got so tired of it that he could hardly stand to continue to eat it for the calories he needed each day. After that experience on the PCT, he never ate gorp again. In later years he really regretted not being able to enjoy it anymore. That was a lesson for both of us, to be sure to include variety in all our food. I had always preferred variety anyway, but now I saw it was important.

The three of us trekked on, and we were delighted when we eventually reached a water cache and the road which the guidebook said led to The Bear's PCT Hikers' Oasis in Anza, near where John had left his truck. In response to our cell phone call, Paul "The Bear" drove to the trail to pick us up. He and his wife Ziggy were wonderful hosts, welcoming us to camp behind their house on the large grassy area with other hikers. They introduced us to hot soaks for our feet, a surprisingly refreshing treat. They kept busy during the weeks following ADZPCTKO, when they were visited by many hikers. They also did our laundry, and they served a spaghetti dinner we had not had to carry – we were very grateful. John retrieved his truck from the campground, and I retrieved my next week's food supply which I had stashed in his truck.

Next morning John and Jennie returned to Phoenix while I continued my hike. We had enjoyed our experiences together, and John really hated to stop hiking and leave me alone on the trail. We three had hiked together about 35 miles; John and I had hiked 145 from the border. Each of us felt a sense of accomplishment.

Later, having ascended into pine forest again in the San Jacinto Mountains, I stopped to visit with some hikers taking a break. A young woman complained bitterly about having to climb so high to get up on the mountain crest, while there was perfectly beautiful country to hike in down below. As she gestured back down the mountainside, I exclaimed, "Oh, you wanted to hike the Pacific *Valley* Trail! I think that must be down there somewhere." She managed a weak smile, but she clearly resented the climbing. Like many hikers, I felt committed to hiking the Pacific Crest Trail, wherever it went. Climbing came with the territory.

As I continued, I saw other hikers every day; sometimes I stopped to take a break with them or hiked awhile with a few. I enjoyed the camaraderie, but I found that I particularly enjoyed hiking alone. Setting my own pace, making all my own decisions unaffected by the plans or wishes of others, feeling the satisfaction of assuming responsibility for my own wellbeing in the outdoors on an ongoing basis, all was a new kind of experience for me. In addition, I found that solitude and natural beauty make a fine combination, especially when they are enjoyed away from the distractions of the city. Even a view of distant city lights could reinforce the sense of solitude, as in my campsite one night high on Mt. San Jacinto. I could see the lights of Palm Springs sparkling far below while I enjoyed the wonderful stillness of the forest. My mind was still as well.

Fuller Ridge, the final major hurdle in the San Jacinto Mountains I had read about, was a rocky but not a very icy challenge that year. Most of the snow had already melted. Then I plunged almost 8,000 ft. down from the mountains to desert again, passing through every life zone in California but the alpine zone. I would see that latter kind of country only later, in the Sierras.

I was amazed to find a working water faucet at the foot of the mountain. I made my way through the desert to Interstate 10 and the Southern Pacific Railroad. I had eaten almost all of my freeze-dried food, so I gladly made my way a short distance along paved Tamarack Road to a restaurant where I could enjoy a hearty lunch. Then it was time to get to the nearby town of Banning to resupply, clean up and do some laundry, and I needed a ride.

I could not remember when I had last asked a stranger for a ride, but I read that it was standard procedure for PCT hikers. I looked around the restaurant and settled on a well-dressed African American man finishing his meal. I quickly finished my own meal and met the man at the cash register. After he paid for his meal, I asked him if he was heading west toward Los Angeles.

The man looked at my scruffy and probably smelly figure and my large backpack, then said he was heading west. I explained that I was hiking the PCT and that I needed a ride to the next town so I could resupply and clean up. To my surprise and relief, he agreed to give me a lift. I paid for my meal, and we left. I told him about my hike as we drove to Banning, and I asked him to drop me off at a motel. He had relaxed as we talked, but he did not seem to fully believe that I was hiking just for the adventure, because when I was about to leave his car he asked me how I was fixed for money! I thanked him very much and assured him that I was fine on that score. I will always regret I did not get his business card so I could send him a postcard at the end of my hike and thank him again.

In my motel room I thoroughly enjoyed a shower then ruefully assessed the large hole I had torn in the seat of my pants. I pinned the tear and then walked a mile to the nearest supermarket where I found food for the next week but no iron-on patches. Neither the grocery cashier nor the motel clerk could tell me where I might find patches within walking distance. I considered my options. Zhita was away on a trip to Mexico with her friend Shirley. But Zhita's daughter Wendy was living in southern California, so I called her to ask for help. She agreed to meet me the next morning. I washed my clothes in the bathtub and hung them to dry while I slept soundly in a bed that night.

Next morning Wendy dropped what she was doing, took her daughter Zhita Lynne with her to buy some iron-on patches and then drove all the way out to Banning to my motel. While I wore a bath towel as a kilt, to young Zhita's amusement, Wendy mended my torn pants. Wendy and Zhita returned me to the trail and then they drove back to their home in Glendale.

Zhita: My Travel Plan

Since Jim is gone, marching off into the wilderness on his own terms, without a way for us to make contact, no way for me to help, guess I might as well go on with my life as usual. There is always plenty to keep me busy. Or I might try an adventure of my own....

My long-time and very special friend, Shirley, is single and always interested in having travel partners. Maybe this is the ideal opportunity. I talk with Shirl and she comes up with a travel plan that sounds ideal to me. There is an Elderhostel trip scheduled for a few weeks hence—while Jim will still be on the trail—that will take us to the center of Mexico—Guanajuato, Queretero, and San Miguel de Allende. It will focus on the culture of these areas, the history and the arts. Wonderful! Perhaps I can even practice a bit of the Spanish that I learned in high school and college. And Shirl would be such a great travel companion. We make our plans....

The trip is ideal; I love the things I see, the things I am learning, the richness of the culture and, of course, Shirley's friendship. But I wonder about Jim—Where is he? How is he doing? When will he return? And then one morning, I get a phone call—completely unexpected—from my daughter Deb. She has heard from her sister Wendy about Jim's need for help on the trail. Hiking in an area southeast of LA, he had a small emergency—a tear in an unfortunate place on his only pair of hiking pants. He had gotten off the trail and hiked to a place where he could make a phone call. Wendy, who lived in Glendale at the time, and granddaughter, Zhita, came to the rescue bringing iron-on patches to make the repair. A small emergency, but I had not been there to help.... I finished the rest of my travels with a bit less enthusiasm, some anxiety and a resolve for the future. This plan would not work again. In future, we would have to find some better way for Jim to communicate. And I would be reachable and available to help.

Jim

From the desert floor, not too far from the road to Palm Springs, the trail begins the ascent up Mt. San Gorgonio. Camping that night well above the private Whitewater fishing preserve, I looked at the expanse of dry grasses on the slopes around me and was reminded of what I thought were scary-looking alcohol stoves with a precarious open can to hold the burning fuel. They were becoming popular among ultralight hikers. Later I learned that just a couple of days after I camped there a hiker spilled his flaming alcohol stove on that grassy slope and set off a wildfire. I was glad I carried the added weight of my more manageable MSR Whisperlite stove with its sealed white gas container.

After hiking into the mountains above 8,500 ft. near Big Bear Lake, I reached Van Dusen Canyon Road. I set down my pack and stuck out my thumb, looking for a ride to Big Bear City where I could resupply again. Soon a car with a bicycle on top stopped, and the driver gave me a ride. He turned out to be an adventure racer, well known in a career I was not even aware of. Paul made his living racing in triathlons and other races, on foot or on bicycle, swimming or kayaking or whatever muscle-powered travel was required. Sponsors who market related gear and food helped make that lifestyle possible. We talked as he drove, and he invited me to stay at his house. He proved to be a very gracious host.

Paul showed me the guest room and bath, and he urged me to give him my laundry to begin washing while I showered. He loaned me clean clothes to wear until the laundry was finished. I was chagrined to discover when I removed my boots and socks that my feet stank terribly. Paul noticed. He urged me to put my leather and fabric boots into the washing machine with my clothes. Convinced that my boots needed to be cleaned but dubious about the method, I tossed them into the washer. I was greatly relieved to find that the boots dried okay afterwards while stuffed with newspaper, apparently none the worse for the treatment. And they certainly smelled better. After that experience, I developed a routine of washing myself every night on the trail, a basic "spit bath" in my tent using a soapy washcloth and an insulated mug of warm water saved from the water I boiled for my dinner. Since I was carrying an extra two pairs of socks and briefs, I could change after bathing, and I stopped every couple of days to rinse out my changes of clothes. No more stink (as far as I could tell).

Just as I stepped out of the shower, Paul urgently called for me to come out to the front of the house. Wrapped in the towel, I stepped outside to see that a young black bear was in the back of Paul's pickup in the driveway, busily ripping open bags and foraging. Paul explained that there was no garbage collection on unpaved portions of streets in Big Bear City, so he kept his bags of garbage in the truck ready for his weekly trip to the dump. The bear smelled food in the tightly closed bags, so he boldly made his way into the residential neighborhood in broad daylight, clambered into the truck and began helping himself. My first wild bear encounter, though it was hardly in the wilderness. I could see how the town got its name.

Paul returned me to the trail the next day, refreshed and resupplied, and I continued hiking north and then west in the San Gabriel Mountains. I looked down to my left on Big Bear Lake as I enjoyed hiking through the Jeffrey Pine and juniper clad mountains at a comfortable pace at around 7,500 ft. I met a few young hikers who had stopped to enjoy the hot springs near the trail along the way, but I was leery of the springs because of the PCT guidebook's caution about possible bacteria colonies in them.

The sense of adventure on my hike was heightened when I met a hiker who told me the PCT was closed ahead because of a wildfire. He said he had been accosted from a low-flying helicopter the day before and told to leave the area, so he turned back. As I approached Silverwood Lake State Recreation Area I saw a sign stating that the trail was closed. I don't remember the details, but it stated there was a hefty fine for defying the closure. I soon found a scrawled sign with instructions for getting off the trail to hitch or hike on a paved highway for miles to bypass the closed area. Stopping to study the sky and the land around me, I saw no smoke or fire or any hint of a burn.

Again and again I hesitated. I had met no hikers who had either skipped around or hiked through the closed area, but I did see fresh tracks of hikers ahead of me who had continued northbound on the trail. Still seeing no smoke or fire, I was unsure whether the closure might still be in effect. I hated to miss a major portion of the trail to walk on a deserted paved road. I decided to take my chances and keep walking cautiously until I saw further cause for alarm. Wildfires are extremely dangerous, of course, and I did not want to take a serious risk or to endanger others who try to rescue hapless hikers in harm's way. I continued to see no fire or smoke anywhere, and no helicopter appeared to warn me away. I trekked on without any problem. Silverwood Lake was closed when I got there, so I was not able to feast on the hotdogs I had looked forward to. Still there was no further indication of a fire anywhere I could see.

I remember well how glad I was the next day to see, at last, the McDonald's I had read about at Cajon Pass. At this point the trail passes under Interstate 15 and some railroad tracks a little below the pass, the highway slicing through the scrubby trees covering the mountains with just this spot of civilization at the pass above me. I made my way off the trail and up to the isolated restaurant and gas station beside the highway at the top of the pass. It was a rare treat to be able to walk less than a mile off the trail to a fast food place, and for once I did not begrudge walking the extra distance away from my goal.

With cellphone coverage along the highway, I called Zhita to tell her I was on schedule to meet her the next day. Then, when I sat down with my long-anticipated large double cheeseburger, large fries and milkshake I was amazed that I could not quite finish the fries. Big as my appetite was, my stomach could not hold all that feast plus a substantial quantity of water. It was getting late as I refilled my water containers and returned to the trail. (I always delighted in "easy" water that I did not have to pump through my filter.) I passed under the highway and some railroad tracks before I decided to stop at a small clearing and make camp in the gathering darkness.

Sleeping in Cajon Canyon turned out to be more memorable than eating at McDonalds. I discovered that I was camped near tracks which were raised about 20 feet above my tent. Freight trains laboriously made their way up to and over the pass every hour or two. I looked out of my tent to see just how close a noisy train was, and I believe I could have thrown a rock and hit the engineer. I felt like doing just that before the night was over.

Next morning I made a groggy start and before long discovered that I was several miles short of where I had intended to camp. That was a problem, because I was to meet Zhita in Wrightwood, a small town just off the trail. I had told her I planned to meet her at about 5:00, but now I would be more than an hour late. As usual, I had no cell phone coverage. I picked up the pace hiking up Wright Mountain, and in a few miles I discovered what shin splints feel like. The thin muscles of my shins were in good condition for hiking at my usual pace, but I had not trained for hurrying uphill with a pack. Sore shin muscles soon were joined by cramps in my calves, and together they hobbled my hiking. Finally I reached the top of the mountain and then the Acorn Trail, branching off to the right, much later than I had planned. Descending that trail down the mountain to town was pretty painful with my sore shins.

Zhita: Meeting in Wrightwood

I was really looking forward to meeting Jim in Wrightwood. This was a charming little village that we had visited as tourists in the past. I knew my way; I drove into town with confidence, then looked at the PCT guide book directions that Jim had printed for me and set out to find the Acorn Trail.

This should be easy. Wrong again.... I asked around at various shops, gas stations, looked for signage; no luck. An inspiration! Surely the crew at the Fire Station would know; they have to be completely familiar with the area so they can rescue people or fight fires wherever they occur. Wrong again.... I left dejected but decided to try following the PCT plan as far as I could and then just hope for the best.

I drove again as far as I could to the area indicated, and saw again the sign that said PRIVATE NO TRESPASSING! What should I do? The road ahead was clearly for automobile use, there were homes at intervals along the way, and I could not see that I would be doing any harm. I needed to rush to meet Jim when he was expected. I drove to the end of the road which stopped at the edge of the forest and parked on the side. I sat and waited and waited—until the owner of the nearby house came home, saw me sitting in the car, and angrily asked that I leave. I explained why I was there and that I would be leaving as soon as my husband arrived. She was insistent; I could not stay there; this was a PRIVATE road! I turned around and drove back slowly, trying to figure out what to do. Meanwhile the time was passing and there was no sign of Jim.

I drove back to the PRIVATE sign and waited—and waited—and waited. It began to get dark; it was now hours past when Jim was due. What could have happened? What were my alternatives? No matter how I tried to figure it out there seemed nothing for me to do but wait.... As dusk arrived and darkness descended, I felt desperate but helpless. And then, I saw the slow movement of a pack-laden man on the road, walking very slowly but walking steadily in my direction. I sprang out of the car; waved my arms and ran up the private road to meet him. What initial joy!!! And then, what shock, as I realized how exhausted and in pain he was. But the greatest shock came after we reached our motel and Jim undressed to take a bath.... I have never seen anyone looking so emaciated! Transformed from the robust man I had seen just days before to someone whom I could only compare to the images I have seen of World War II concentration camp survivors. The skin was literally hanging off his body... But he was my Jim and he was safe and we were together. And, of course, he would continue hiking.

Jim

When Zhita exclaimed that I looked emaciated, I said I was eager to get to a restaurant to begin to rectify that condition! We celebrated a welcome full day off the next day with more hugs, showers, restaurant meals, and sleeping in a bed. For future hikes I needed to find some way to eat more calories, and we also agreed we needed to find better ways to communicate while I was on my trek.

Next morning my painful shin splints led me to change my mind about returning to the PCT by hiking back up the Acorn Trail to the top of Mt. Wrightwood. Instead I carefully drove us up a rutted dirt road to meet the PCT about 3 miles west of its junction with the Acorn Trail and down from the mountain. I left Zhita with the hazardous drive in our Camry back down that rough road to reach paved roads and civilization, and I hobbled on down the trail.

I made my way slowly until I reached Little Jimmy Campground, where I was glad for the luxury of tables and readymade campsites. On the next day I reached Angeles Crest Hwy 2, where my friend Gene and his friend and neighbor Kim met me to hike with me for a few miles. For this first year on the PCT I had chosen Islip Saddle as a place where Gene could hike with me not too far from his home in Los Angeles and on a day he could get free. Gene and Kim did not mind my slow pace, so we hiked together several miles through white firs and ceanothus to the place where they had left Kim's car so they could drive back to Gene's car parked at our meeting place. I really enjoyed hiking together with them, even though I was too distracted by my sore legs to be a very cheery companion. We said goodbye, and I hobbled on.

On my third day of hiking painfully slowly, I realized that I could not reach Agua Dulce on the day I had arranged to meet Zhita there for the end of this year's hike. My cell phone had no coverage where I was, as usual, and I had no way to communicate with her. If I continued, she would be very worried when I did not show up. I decided to bail out at the unoccupied Mill Creek Summit Ranger Station next to the Angeles

Forest Highway. There I gave the bulk of my newly opened half pound of cheese to another hiker, and I went out on the road to hitch a ride.

A family stopped their car and asked where I was going. I assured them my wife would come to get me anywhere it was convenient for them to take me in the greater LA area. They took me to their party supply shop in Highland Park. While Rosa drove, she and I carried on a conversation in awkward English about my hike and her commute to work, while her husband and her father communicated in Spanish. When we arrived at their shop, I sat on the sidewalk in front of the store and called Zhita. She dropped everything to come and find me. While I waited, Rosa bought a cup of hot cocoa and a pan dulce at a nearby shop and brought the treat to me. Zhita arrived soon after. We exclaimed our gratitude to Rosa and returned home on Saturday, May 22.

I had hiked about 420 miles on my first venture on the Pacific Crest Trail. Though humbled by my discovered limitations, I exulted in my achievement. All things considered, it was a fine hike and a fine adventure.

In July my younger daughter Kirsten and I returned to the spot on the PCT near Wrightwood where Zhita and I parted after my day off. We hiked together from that dirt road up to the Acorn Trail junction and then back again so I could see the bit of trail I had skipped when my shin muscles hurt so. Kirsten was delighted to take a token hike with me on the PCT and thus participate in my adventure. Even brief hikes with loved ones and friends became treasured bright spots among my trove of memories from my epic journey.

2005 Experience

There are three kinds of men. The ones that learn by readin.' The few who learn by observation. The rest of them have to pee on the electric fence for themselves.

WILL ROGERS

April

This year I knew a little better what I was doing in preparing for hiking. My first long hike in 2004 had taught me some new ideas, disabused me of some illusions and bad ideas, and reinforced the value of some things I had learned from reading and from my limited prior experience. I would learn more this year, particularly about my own limitations, but I certainly would benefit from what I learned last year. Less ignorance, more knowledge. I was eager to begin.

John and I would start by attending ADZPCTKO again this year, then driving to the town of Agua Dulce afterwards to begin our hike. The guidebook cautioned that by June the temperatures in the desert north of town would range around 100 degrees, and we wanted to hike that section before it heated up. We planned to hike this hundred mile stretch together in the spring and then return to the trail going into the Sierras in the fall after the snow melted, taking advantage of the section hiker's flexibility. I had decided to skip for now the part of the trail between Agua Dulce and Mill Creek Summit, where I had stopped the previous year, in order to begin with John in a more convenient location. I would hike the skipped part later.

My detailed hike plan had been a winner for me last year, so it remained an important part of my planning and preparing. I spent more days doing training hikes this year to better toughen my feet as well as my muscles. That toughening plus more liberal use of petroleum jelly would limit blisters on my feet.

I had learned that I needed to eat more calories, so I decided to buy commercial freeze-dried dinners for two so I wouldn't lose so much weight on the trail. Last year I was unable to eat all the energy bars and snack food I carried, but since I still had a hearty appetite for dinner, I thought I could manage to eat more then. I also wanted more satisfying dinners to alternate with the commercial hikers' meals, and I settled on buying bulk cans of freeze-dried vegetables and pre-cooked meats and combining double portions of them in freezer bags. Tough freezer bags are FDA rated for heating frozen food in a microwave, so the bags seemed safe enough for holding boiling water added to a meal. Instant brown rice and other starches provided a choice of bases, adding needed calories. Such meals would be almost as simple to use on the trail as commercial hikers' dinners, and they would be much less trouble to prepare beforehand than, say, dehydrating meals cooked at home. Experimenting with sauces and spices from different cultures offered plenty of variety.

In one final preparation before beginning this year's hike, Zhita and I drove to Agua Dulce for lunch and then set out seeking three locations in the arid landscape ahead where I wanted to leave a small water cache near the trail, just in case. Since we were in the area of the coming hike, I also brought a box holding six commercial freeze-dried dinners to store for John and myself at what was known as Hikertown, the residence of Jack Fair in Antelope Valley where many hikers took a welcome break. John and I had learned to appreciate any opportunity to postpone carrying even a little weight.

Over the Hill

After some searching we found the sites where I planned to hide my water bottles. When we drove to Hikertown to leave the box of food, the men we met there were quite agreeable to holding the box for me even though it was clear that this was not something they were used to doing. One offered to keep my box under his bed so other hikers would not think the food was discarded and help themselves.

This year Zhita persuaded me to rent a satellite phone to carry. I had resisted because the phones then available weighed almost a pound, and because they were very expensive. I said I relented so she would sleep better while I was hiking, but I also knew I would be safer with the phone, especially when hiking alone. It certainly would be an advantage to have the phone if I needed to tell her of an unexpected change in plans. I picked up the "sat phone" on Thursday, the day before I left for the hike. I had spent the day Wednesday working with my map software, with moderate success, so this time I completed printing my maps before my departure day. I had learned not to print so many pages of detailed maps. I went through my check list for filling my pack and then also reviewed my new separate check list for departure (loaded backpack, maps and guidebook pages for my pockets, hat, trekking poles, and *boots*). The departure list was a safeguard against last-minute distractions such as I experienced last year. No more setting out without boots.

John and I met at Lake Morena Campground for ADZPCTKO on April 23. Once again I enjoyed talking to many hikers about what they looked forward to and what this long hike meant to them. I found much diversity among the enthusiastic, mostly much younger hikers. The most common theme I heard was the great adventure of such a challenging long hike, and an unspoken but evident theme was taking on responsibility for themselves. I talked about my own more modest plans and expectations, and John added his own perspective in our conversations. We both were buoyed by the contagious enthusiasm.

For this year's Kickoff I was prepared with a little "invention" which I could enter, tongue in cheek, in the annual contest for new gadgets or techniques which were offered as something useful for hikers.

Remembering the spectacle John and I had observed on the trail last year as a young man had struggled hopelessly with his mylar covered umbrella, advocated by ultralight guru Ray Jardine, I had devised an even lighter, more practical shield against the weather. I had gotten a small sheet of mylar at a plastics store, cut out a piece to fit the flat top of my hiking hat and glued it on the hat. For a flexible weatherproof glue, I thinned clear GE Silicone II with mineral spirits and then applied it with a small disposable paintbrush.

I couldn't have asked for a better setup for my entry in the contest. I saw a young man who had devised an umbrella holder upon his backpack's shoulder strap, using a piece of water pipe insulation and lots of duct tape. He proudly wore his pack sporting his mylar-covered umbrella which sheltered him from rain and sun a la Ray Jardine. I just knew he would enter that in the contest. When I asked the organizer when the contest would begin, he offered to let me be first. I urged that he let the man with the umbrella contraption go first and then I would follow. It was perfect.

The young man demonstrated to the crowd the complicated way he could mount his umbrella in its holder and then get his pack on his back without damaging the umbrella or poking out his eye. Once his pack and umbrella finally were mounted, he could hike with his umbrella upright and both hands free for his trekking poles. When someone in the audience asked him to demonstrate again how to install the umbrella in the holder, he said "Oh no, it's too much trouble! I have to take my pack off carefully and get the umbrella out, then install the umbrella again and get the pack on again…" Instead he just went through the motions and reminded us of how he had done it initially.

Then it was my turn. I demonstrated my wide-brimmed hat with its ventilated crown and shiny top, a gentle spoof on the mylar umbrella. I simply put my hat on, so the mylar would reflect a tiny bit of heat or deflect a bit of rain, keeping my head shaded and cool and my eyeglasses clear of the rain. Both hands were free for my trekking poles, and wind would not be a problem. I had to use my hat's chin strap (a long piece of boot lace) when the wind blew, but I never feared that the hat would turn inside out.

My entry won all of two votes for best invention (my own vote and my brother's, who said he voted for me because my invention was the only one he understood), so I was the last contestant to go to the table of donated prizes and select one. Later in the chilly, windy evening a young hiker called out to ask me if my head was still cool. My ventilated hat was not so advantageous in the cold. Much later – too late for a snappy comeback – I thought I should have joked that I would next devise a way to tie my stove windbreak around the crown of my hat when there was a cold wind.

John and I learned from Meadow Ed's water report at ADZPCTKO that spring of 2005 was a pretty good season for hikers to find water in the usual sources along the PCT in southern California. My water caches were not likely to be needed. Oh well, we had the comfort of being sure we could get water in some places where the guidebook cautioned that the water supply was uncertain or nonexistent. On the other hand, we were glad we were not hiking over nearby Mt. San Jacinto that year, as the snow there was reported to be pretty deep.

On Sunday John and I each drove to Agua Dulce where we found Hiker Heaven, the home of the famous trail angels Donna and Jeff Saufley. We arranged to leave our vehicles in their large enclosed yard while we hiked. We stayed that night in their generous dormitory quarters for hikers passing through, enjoying their hospitality and the camaraderie of the other hikers there. We discovered that Donna had arranged to pick up some hikers at the Tehachapi – Willow Springs Road where we planned to finish this section hike. She would meet the hikers next Sunday, the very day we would arrive there, so she cheerily offered to pick us up as well and return us all to her home. That saved us from driving both of our vehicles to Tehachapi to leave one and driving back to the Saufley's to begin our hike, so we were delighted to accept Donna's offer.

In the morning we set out, walking north on Agua Dulce Canyon Road out of town. We started on Monday at Trail Mile 455. On a series of paved roads, unpaved jeep roads and trail tread we hiked through the chamise chaparral. From the town the trail winds up through the transverse mountain range and then down to cross the western arm of the Mojave Desert in the Antelope Valley. PCT trail construction standards call for a cleared tread, or pathway, three feet wide with a limited grade up or down hill, and minimal irregularities of stones, roots or crevices, affording hikers and horses alike safe passage. The standards set a goal, not always realized. Where the trail simply followed a road, more or less temporarily, the roadbed might be more variable. We earnestly hoped the PCT could someday be routed around all this developed land to better realize the wild scenes and experiences which make the trail so rewarding to travel.

We enjoyed getting water from my caches which required no filtering, and it was easy to carry the flattened containers, leaving no trace. But to our amazement, somewhere along the way we came upon a grinning "life-sized" plastic skeleton tied to a bush, outfitted with a bandana around its neck and another as a loincloth. It marked an oasis devised by a trail angel for the refreshment of hikers. The oasis was a shaded little glen nestled in the tall ceanothus bushes, decorated with the skeleton and a pink plastic flamingo and furnished with folding chairs and a large cooler filled with water. It was a luxury to take a break in shaded chairs with back support while drinking a cold soda which we had not carried. Still, the scene was a startling contrast with the desert landscape through which the PCT was taking us, which is what we were here for.

While hiking in the Sawmill Mountains we occasionally had views of the Antelope Valley and beyond it to the Tehachapi Mountains. The trail tread in this area was good, well-worn dirt with a sprinkling of rock and an occasional root. I generally looked where I was walking pretty regularly, but once I stubbed my toe on a root and pitched forward. I dropped my poles and reached out to break my fall with both hands, but with the weight on my back my arms were not able to even slow me down. I landed flat on my face with a splat, surprisingly without breaking or even damaging anything. I fumbled with efforts to get up with the weight on my back, finally clambering into a sitting position so I could remove my pack. I wiped the dirt from my face, examining and then carefully readjusting my glasses. I was sore (nose, lips, and chin) but not bleeding or damaged. John was relieved to see that I wasn't hurt. Only my dignity, I assured him.

We came to a trail junction that was pretty confusing. The scene with its one surviving sign did not appear to correspond with any guidebook description. We had been heading west in the Sawmill Mountains, but I knew we soon needed to head north toward Antelope Valley. After some discussion we decided to take the trail to the right. Later we found that we had taken the correct fork. We met up with a couple of hikers who had just hitched a ride on the nearby highway to get back to the PCT. They had taken the other fork at the confusing junction and hiked several miles on some other trail. We speculated about whether a sign had been deliberately relocated or hidden by vandals in order to make it difficult for PCT hikers.

When the guys heard about my recent splat on the trail, they said that they would now have a clue about which way to go: Hereafter they would simply look for Jim's face print on the trail at any junction. We laughed. They soon stopped to camp, and John and I hiked on. At the next few trail junctions I obligingly used my trekking pole to draw a cartoon on the trail, a sprawling stick figure with a flattened face and glasses askew to indicate the right way.

Our descent from the mountains down into the Antelope Valley was memorable. A storm was brewing, and on the ridge where we planned to camp John and I struggled to erect our Tarptents in a strong wind. Even when both of us worked on one tent together we could not do it. Finally we wadded up our tents and strapped them to our packs and descended farther down to find a sheltered spot. It was getting dark when we found a level area among trees, and we set up camp and ate dinner. That night the storm was upon us, and heavy rain was buffeted by the winds which reached us even among the trees. Neither of us slept well, and during the night we struggled repeatedly to get water out of our tents' bathtub floors. In the morning we were cold and thoroughly soaked, along with our sleeping bags and packs. In the daylight we discovered that we were camped in a formerly dry wash, so the ground around us had become a bog.

Mercifully, that was the day we would reach Jack Fair's Hikertown, so we wadded up our wet gear and tied it to our packs. The overgrown grasses and bushes were laden with water, so our pant legs, socks and boots were replenished with as much water as they could hold as we walked. We made our soggy way down into the desert as we entered Antelope Valley, not feeling like desert hikers at all. The wind continued but the water gradually disappeared. After crossing busy Hwy 138, we were relieved to reach Hikertown at last.

A low chain link fence enclosed a yard sparsely covered with sagebrush. Several men lived in the modest main house. They said we could sleep where we liked, in the unoccupied second house which served as a dorm or in the spacious yard. There was an outhouse, a shed and a stack of miscellaneous old lumber and debris in the yard. Paint on the wooden buildings was peeling. We found an empty room in the dorm and proceeded to empty our packs, taking almost everything outside where we spread sleeping bags, tents, packs, etc. on the sage brush to dry in the wind. I found the man who had saved my box of dinners and he returned them to me, remarking as he did how good those hiker's dinners are and how he enjoyed the ones he occasionally found left behind. I was pleased to find the contents of my box intact, especially since I now looked forward to eating a full dinner for two each night! We gave the guy a tip in exchange for a ride to the nearby country store for cold beer and salty snacks.

There was a quirky atmosphere about Hikertown, unlike what we had found at Hiker Heaven or at Hiker's Oasis. A few other hikers spent the night here, but I noticed that several women decided that their groups would move on instead. Next morning I think I discovered why they left. The bathroom in the dorm building had a door of glass panes, with no indication I could see that there had ever been a curtain covering the glass. Sitting there I looked out through the large windows of what had been a living room once, and I was gazing into the driveway just a few feet beyond. Not many vehicles drove in or out on that once-graveled drive, but I mused whether I would wave if anyone did go by. I was glad that no one walked into the living room to see whether the bathroom was occupied.

Another disquieting feature of the place was the sign in one room that said something to the effect that the best thing about life was the ability to end it at a time of one's own choosing. (I read in a later year that Jack Fair, once the owner of the place, had in fact ended his own life with his revolver in 2001.)

John and I made good use of our time at Hikertown, especially because we were able to dry our down sleeping bags rather well in the unceasing desert wind. Packs, tents, everything but our boots were pretty well restored to a suitable condition, and even the boots were much improved. We enjoyed swapping stories with the few other hikers, and a couple of southbound hikers confirmed that the weather was mild for the desert crossing ahead of us. Not the first to leave in the morning, we set out in a much better mood than we had been in when we arrived.

We made our way out of the little community, past the wooden schoolhouse and several houses and paved roads to reach the dirt road that served as the PCT. We exclaimed about our good choice and good fortune to be crossing the desert in such mild weather. We crossed over the concrete-lined river of the California Aqueduct and then followed the trail/road alongside the fully enclosed Los Angeles Aqueduct, sometimes underground in a channel covered by concrete panels and sometimes in a large pipe above ground. We noted the irony of the sound of a torrent of water gurgling through the pipe alongside of hikers who had to stretch the resources of their burdens to last until water was actually accessible. Now we were truly glad we decided to hike this arid section of the trail in the spring, imagining that the gurgling sound might be a torment to thirsty hikers in summer's desert heat.

For many years the Tejon Ranch Company refused to allow the PCT to cross its large property, which includes much of the Tehachapi Mountains in southern California. The company owners finally consented to let the trail use a narrow corridor along the southeast corner of its land, allowing the trail to access the Mojave Desert in Antelope Valley as an alternative to the mountain route originally envisioned. In recent years, however, the company sought to develop a new town and industry on its land, requiring a lot of permits as well as support from area governments and taxpayers for connecting roads, water and power, etc. To avoid many years of litigation which would naturally be required to get such extensive cooperation and support, the company negotiated agreements with a group of environmental organizations as well as with the governments and businesses involved. The company's concession which pleases me most is allowing the PCT to be routed along the crest of the Tehachapi Mountains, the original intent of the trail's planners. Someday I hope to be able to help with trail construction on the mountain trail which will replace the present route of the PCT through the Mojave Desert in Antelope Valley.

We wound our way on sandy dirt roads and on up into the Tehachapi foothills at last, angered at times by the sight of wide-spread destruction by dirt bikes and ATVs. Many times it appeared that the riders must have taken perverse glee in tearing up as much soil as possible, digging ruts and spewing soil and sparse vegetation far and wide. Then making our way through a wind farm among the giant towers of wind generators and the occasional big blades lying on the ground, we mused about the chances of happening by a tower when its blades fell off.

At the higher elevation the wind turned cold. We were thoroughly chilled in the early morning of the day we were to meet the hikers being picked up by Donna. John walked ahead of me, and I was surprised to hear an involuntary yelp. I looked up to see him in a very funny leap. He did a one-legged hop in midstride because he saw a coiled snake where he was about to step. It turned out to be a Green Mojave Rattlesnake, and John just missed stepping on it. We guessed that the snake had emerged from some hole to get into the sunlight, but it was still too cold for the reputedly aggressive snake to be active. It did not stir as we took pictures, and we moved on. We were now notably livelier than the snake.

Coming off the windswept ridge, we followed the trail down to Oak Creek, where we filtered our last few liters of water for this trek. With time to spare, we walked down the trail to the crossing with paved Tehachapi-Willow Springs Road at Mile 555. We dropped our packs in the dirt parking area beside the road. Soon we were joined by three other hikers and then by Donna in her SUV. On our way back to Agua Dulce we stopped at a store to buy refreshments and then again at a roadside stand to buy flats of strawberries. We all were delighted to arrive at Hiker Heaven. John and I agreed that we had enjoyed a good hike together, with no real complaints. We set out for home in our respective vehicles, John declining to drive into Los Angeles to spend the night with me and Zhita before heading for Phoenix. We enjoyed our camaraderie on the trail together, but John had no patience for driving in LA's traffic.

Spring desert hiking behind us, we looked forward to fall and the Sierras. We had hiked another 100 miles on the PCT.

Fall 2005

With hiking as my main focus now, I did not sign up for any art classes in the fall. After more months of planning, preparing and especially training, Zhita returned me to the trail at Tehachapi-Willow Springs Road near Tehachapi Pass on Friday, August 5. I began my hike alone. I was pleased that my pack's base weight was 29 lbs.; total weight including food and water was 49 lbs. That was an improvement over what I started with in the spring, so I was making a little progress. On Saturday the temperature was in the upper 90's, and I ran out of water during an exposed 2,000ft climb. I ran out of water on Sunday, too, but I rationed my water much better through more of the day.

Rationing water is always a cautious experiment for me, as I need to keep hydrated so I can reach the next water source. I read that Search and Rescue teams sometimes find people recently dead of dehydration who still had water enough to have survived until rescued. They evidently had been saving their water for when they felt more in need, not realizing how dehydrated they already were. (I haven't read of any such tragedies on the PCT.) I do fine hiking in the heat when I have plenty of water, but I have to slow down and rest more when I run low or out of it. I planned for the dry stretches, but of course caution is necessary, as the guidebook and other sources of information about the PCT strongly advise.

On Sunday I reached Robin Bird Spring late and tired, so I simply drank plenty of water and went to sleep. I ate Sunday's dinner for breakfast on Monday and set out in morning's more hospitable weather. I worked out a good system for efficient resting while hiking in the heat. I hiked for an hour, then stopped and took off my boots and socks to cool off for a 20 minute break. I laid down with feet slightly elevated, if possible, and on the hottest days I took off my pants and shirt and lay on them, clad only in briefs. I did not see another hiker in those five days.

I was unable to make up for my short mileage on the first 2 days of this stretch, so on Wednesday I hiked about 21 miles to reach Zhita at Walker Pass. The long day's hike ensured that I did not reach Walker Pass by 5:00, as planned.

Zhita's Story 2005 April

Year Two!!! We have learned a lot from Year One. Most gratifying to me is that my beloved will now carry a satellite phone. I know it adds to the weight that he must carry, and we both regret that; but it will allow us to connect—even from the trail—at least most of the time. (Of course, we will learn more....)

2005 Fall Walker Pass

And that learning begins during the Fall segment of this year's hike with our first scheduled meet-up at Walker Pass... Based on our phone conversation the evening before, Jim expected to reach the meeting place at 5pm. Of course, I wanted to make sure to be there when he arrived, so I left plenty of driving time and arrived at about 3:30. I drove the Explorer in case the campground area roads were rough. Lovely area with camping facilities and smooth roads, but deserted at this time of day. I parked the car, wandered a bit, tried to imagine just where Jim would emerge. As the time wore on, I was happy to take advantage of the restroom facility. I returned and waited.... and waited... and waited. No sign of Jim. As night began to fall, I realized how helpless I was. I didn't have cell phone reception in the area. Was I waiting in the right place? If I left to search elsewhere, I might still not be able to make or receive a call–and still not know if I had found the intended meeting place. Nothing for me to do but wait and wait... and worry. I also managed to add some anxiety of my own....

Sitting in the car, I began searching through my purse for some reason. OMG! My wallet was missing!!! How could that be? I was frantic. Then I remembered, with a sickening feeling, that when I had gone to the restroom I had left my purse in the car—and the car unlocked. There was no sign of people. What could have happened? But the missing wallet was minor compared to my missing husband. What angst....

Then at dusk, like a scene from a movie, a weary figure emerged from the trail!

It was Jim, laden with his pack, obviously exhausted, but joyous. We had connected!!! But the day was not over.... We drove 40 miles, around beautiful Lake Isabella, to the nearest motel. Fortunately, Jim's hiking essentials included one credit card. This allowed us to have dinner of pizza in a deserted restaurant, a good night's sleep and breakfast together before continuing on our separate journeys.

As I drove back to LA, the reality of the lost wallet was my focus. Hoping that I had somehow left it at home, I discovered it sooner than anticipated. Miraculously, it was sitting on the front seat of the unlocked Camry, our other car, where it had fallen out of my purse—exactly as I had left it. I felt that I had navigated an adventure trail of my own.

Jim

Thursday morning I dressed in clean hiking clothes and refilled my pack. I had learned to provide another set of hiking clothes to include with my resupply bag, since washing clothes during my short time off the trail was so inconvenient. I didn't know anyone who enjoyed the wonderful luxury of the support Zhita provided me. We had a generous breakfast at a café and returned to Walker Pass. Again with no other hikers in sight, I kissed her goodbye and started out.

That night I was pleased about outfoxing the mosquitoes, having the zipper closed on my tent before I erected it and then getting everything ready so I could quickly open the zipper and get inside with everything I wanted and close the zipper again before any mosquitoes could follow. Partly luck, I know. Next morning I felt really good, breezing down a cool western slope and seeing the early morning sun shining on the other side of the grassy valley. I began singing *The sun is shining, Oh happy day...*" I called Zhita on the sat phone and left her a message, singing that familiar old song.

Sailing on in my exuberance down the easy slope, I suddenly felt my right knee give way. Only my trekking poles saved me from collapsing on the spot. I guess I was going fast downhill and not bothering to put weight on my poles in order to absorb some of the shock. Finding no apparent damage to my knee, I carefully got to my feet and tried walking cautiously, using my right pole as a cane. I continued walking slowly for a couple of hours, not sure I could trust my knee to support me. I felt no pain, so I decided to continue cautiously until either I felt it was safe to continue my hike or else to call Zhita and find a road where I could bail out to get to a doctor. I had never experienced such a dramatic failure of my knee, and I didn't know what to expect. The day had started so wonderfully, and then I thought my hiking career was over, at least for this year. What a disappointment.

Next day I wrapped my knee in an elastic bandage, just in case. I continued walking carefully and had no further mishap. Gradually I felt relieved. Then on the uphill slopes approaching Kennedy Meadows I felt more confident. On Sunday I reached Kennedy Meadows where I would meet Zhita. I was glad to see people, after once again having seen no other hiker during my last 5 days on the trail. When I reached the campground I had hiked just over 50 more miles since Walker Pass.

Zhita and I found each other in spite of the very long campground and its limited signage. She had driven the Explorer this time, as we planned to sleep in the back of it. It would be her first experience camping out. We went to the General Store for lunch, and I took a shower in an outdoor roofless stall. Then we drove to a campsite where we intended to spend the night. As I was setting up our air mattresses and sleeping bags, clouds of mosquitoes began driving us crazy. We managed to eat the picnic supper she had brought while we sat enclosed in the truck, but I did not want to try our little adventure of sleeping out where the mosquitoes were so bad. It would be no fun to go out during the night to pee. We decided to leave. We packed up and drove 50 miles down from the mountains to a little town in the valley far below with the unlikely name of Ridgecrest. The motel room there was a welcome alternative to the mountains with mosquitoes. The sky now appeared dark and stormy.

When we arrived back at Kennedy Meadows on Monday morning, we found that there had been a major thunderstorm in our absence.

Sleeping in the lowlands turned out to have been our best choice. I set out refreshed and resupplied, while Zhita returned home.

Hiking in the famed Sierra high country at last, I really enjoyed the spectacular view of the mountains to the north, though I often stopped to catch my breath. Once I had to step aside from the trail while three cowboys on horseback passed by with assorted dogs and about 30 head of cattle, moving down to a lower pasture for the coming winter. I continued climbing, making my way through the sagebrush meadow back into pines and junipers.

Soon I met Tom from Texas, going the same direction as I was but a little faster. I was focused on my slow pace and not thinking about tomorrow yet. We hiked together for a couple of miles, past Chicken Spring Lake to a spot 12 miles from Crabtree Meadow where the trail to Mt. Whitney branched off. We camped near a stream, and I saw that Tom carried the same type of water filter as I had left at home for this part of the trail. I had reduced my pack weight a little by substituting iodine tablets for the filter, but the treated water tasted pretty bad. Tom generously let me borrow his filter so I could enjoy some clean tasting water. Next morning Tom was on his way before I finished loading my pack, but I expected to see him again as we both planned to hike the side trip to the top of Mt. Whitney.

When I reviewed my progress, using my mileage notes in my trail guide pages, I found that I had been hiking only 10 to 12 miles per day. The thin air at the 10,000 – 11,000 ft. altitude must have slowed me down, making me stop to catch my breath an extra hour or two each day. Hello, thin air! My hike plan was laid out with the assumption that I would hike at least 15 miles per day, but apparently my lungs did not permit that here.

My brother and Jennie had arranged to join me far ahead at Red's Meadow, but I could not hike that far at this altitude in time to meet them as scheduled. I had to make a drastic change in my hike plan. I called Zhita on the sat phone to tell her of the change, as now I would next meet her a day later than planned, go home for a few days and then skip ahead on the trail. My newly discovered limitation was very disappointing. On the other hand, since there was no new damage or danger due to hiking at altitude that I could see, I need not give up on hiking in the Sierras. I would simply accommodate to my newfound limits by allowing more time, and I could continue to hike the PCT.

I also had to skip Mt. Whitney now, very disappointing since I was acclimated as well as I could be and I had my Whitney permit. I was prepared, except that I did not have enough food to take that side trip and continue on to Kearsarge Pass and down to Onion Valley where Zhita would meet me. In fact, I really didn't have enough food to comfortably reach Zhita at my new pace even without the side trip to Mt. Whitney. I had been looking forward to seeing the view from the 14,505 ft. peak, but it was not to be this time. I found a place to camp, and I shed my pack.

Soon I was joined by Nancy and Linda, young northbound section hikers. They decided to camp nearby. When they learned about my situation, they very generously insisted on sharing their dinner with me, and they also filtered water for me. Unexpected trail angels in such a remote location... I was very appreciative. We enjoyed visiting a bit before getting into our tents, and they were gone when I got up in the morning.

The next night I camped near some little lakes above tree line on the approach to Forester Pass. I tried fishing in the rocky pools a little while, but I didn't get a bite. I could see small fish, but I couldn't make my salmon eggs alluring to them. So much for my experiment with carrying fishing gear and a fishing license. Next morning I trekked to the pass with no trouble apart from panting for oxygen, there being only a little well-trodden snow and ice on the trail. The views were spectacular at Forester Pass, the high point on the PCT at 13,180 ft. Even so, it seemed somewhat anticlimactic reach the pass without the legendary challenge of snow and ice fields on the trail I had read about. All I had to contend with were occasional icy snow patches and an inordinate amount of huffing and puffing.

As I took a short break on the north side of the pass, a voice called out behind me, "Hey, I saw you at the Kick Off!" I looked up to see a young would-be through hiker who would not reach Canada before the snow flew. He recognized my shiny-topped hat, he explained. He had hiked all the way from Mexico, at a faster pace than mine, but he had taken time off to attend a family member's funeral. We talked about his falling behind his original plan and his current hopes for getting as far as Washington, at least, before the snow got too deep. I told him I had to compromise even for my much more modest goal for the year.

I decided I could hike up Mt. Whitney another time, based on my success in reaching Forester Pass. If I were suitably acclimated and then carried only a day pack for the last part of the Whitney climb – and if I allowed extra time for huffing and puffing – I could do it. "I'll be back" I pledged to myself.

I met Tom again on the way to Vidette Meadow. He had made the side trip and hiked to the top of Mt. Whitney. I was impressed and envious, but Tom made light of his accomplishment. We hiked together to the top of Bubbs Creek Canyon. He figured he hiked about a third faster than I did at that altitude, so he was going on ahead of me. Since he would be taking a break to resupply in Independence, down below Kearsarge Pass, I urged him to look for Zhita at the parking lot in Onion Valley. If he did not get a ride to town before I arrived, we would take him.

The trail to Kearsarge Pass leaves the PCT at trail mile 784, and then I had nine more miles to go to reach Zhita. I hiked up to the pass at 11,760 ft. with no particular trouble and descended about 3,000 ft. to Onion Valley. On the way down I met a hiker even older than I who was climbing up alone with a nearly empty pack. He was proud of the pack, which he had designed and sewn himself to fit on an old Kelty pack frame. We talked briefly, and I learned that he was 84 years old. In preparation for a backpacking trip to celebrate his upcoming 85th birthday, he was returning over the pass to a spot near Bullfrog Lake to retrieve a food stash from an earlier year. I was surprised that he expected to find the stash intact and the food still edible. He assured me that he had buried the food deep enough that no bear would disturb it and that he knew from past experience that the freeze-dried food would still be good. Amazed, I wished him well and continued down the trail to the parking lot in Onion Valley.

There I found my beloved Zhita and also Tom. Zhita had brought a couple of beers for me, so I gave one to Tom. Soon we drove down the winding road to Independence where we dropped Tom off at his motel, then continued on to the motel Zhita had reserved for us. I took a welcome shower, and we had a hearty lunch at Carl's Jr. I took a nap, and then we went out for dinner. How I enjoyed eating meals freshly cooked by someone else!

On our way home to Los Angeles on Tuesday we took advantage of our free time together and stopped to visit Manzanar, the concentration camp for Americans of Japanese descent during World War II. We found it moving, troubling to see the monument to such a racist, unjust use made of a remote wild area in our nation's past. We felt the irony of their imprisonment near where hikers today enjoy such freedom. We joined countless others in vowing, never again!

Determined to meet John and Jennie far ahead at Red's Meadow on schedule, I recalculated my hike plan to begin next at Lake Edison near trail mile 877 where Zhita could drop me off. Now resigned to my slow pace at about 10,000 ft., I planned the rest of the year's hike with a more realistic goal of about ten miles per day. I appreciated the luxury of being retired and so being able to rearrange my schedule. And I could return another year to see what I was skipping this time in the Sierras. Section hiking the trail was a luxury also because I could choose the season for each section. Getting older was slowing me down, but there was no need to stop.

After preparing my new hike plan, I made some adjustments to the contents of my bags of food for my resupply points each week. Though my hike was being interrupted for only a few days while I was down at sea level, I was well aware of my need to be acclimated to the altitude. I decided that Zhita and I should leave home in time to spend two nights and a day together at Vermillion Valley Resort at Lake Edison at nearly 8,000 ft. before I resumed my hike. That would provide Zhita a rare opportunity to see the spectacular High Sierras where I was hiking.

We left for the mountains on Friday, August 26. Zhita noted that I ate a huge brunch at 11:00 (after our breakfast at home), followed a little later by a huge lunch. Of course I had room for a hearty dinner as well. I did not dare to eat like this apart from hiking.

We were very glad we were forewarned about the rough road from Prather, northeast of Fresno, to the lake. The high clearance of our Explorer was essential, and we were both concerned about Zhita's return drive alone in the big, awkward vehicle on that hazardous drive. This road had been paved long ago, and now the surface was badly broken and potholed. It was very narrow, winding, and often edged by a precipitous drop off. No guardrails, of course. We met no other vehicles.

Our accommodations at the resort turned out to be a travel trailer, 8 by 24 feet. Once long ago I had lived in a trailer like that for a year, so it brought back memories. This one made a comfortable bedroom, and it overlooked the lake. Dinner in the restaurant was remarkably good. The lake was bordered by towering pines, and we sat outside our room after dinner to watch the sunset coloring traces of clouds which were reflected in the lake. Then we moved inside to read, and I reviewed the guidebook description of the trail to come.

On Saturday we took the boat ride to the far end of the lake and back again, relishing the view of the snowcapped mountains to the north and their reflection in the smooth water of the lake. The boat operator pointed out an osprey nest high in a treetop beside the lake, and we watched as an osprey soared out to hunt. Back at the lodge we walked together in the woods (no backpack), relaxed and read. It was a lovely day together in a part of the Sierras that few people get to enjoy unless they reach it on foot or on horseback.

Next morning I was on the boat to return to the other end of the lake, just a few miles from the PCT. I started hiking from the boat landing at

9:30, heading north. I hiked about ten miles, ascending 3,000 ft. and descending 1,000 ft. The next day I hiked over Silver Pass at 10,900 ft. with no more trouble than usual at such an altitude, very reassuring. At one point I met a couple of southbound section hikers and stopped to chat. One man asked how much my pack weighed, and then, "How old are you?" When I told him I was 69 he turned to his partner and exclaimed "There's still hope!" He explained that just before they met me they had been talking about whether they would be able to carry a backpack in their later 50's. They were reassured to think they might have many more years to enjoy hiking.

On Monday I camped just about six miles from Red's Meadow, where I was to meet John and Jennie, on schedule. Next morning I arrived in time to have lunch at the café, then I set up camp and visited my few neighbors in Reds Meadow Campground. John and Jennie arrived in plenty of time to set up camp before we all went to the café for dinner. Tuesday morning I called Zhita while looking over a broad meadow with the early sun gleaming on the heavily frosted grass. I described the sparkling meadow to her, knowing how she enjoyed seeing the morning sun highlight the dew on leaves and grasses at home.

After breakfast the three of us hiked to Devil's Postpile and Rainbow Falls. It was easy walking with no packs, but we could feel the effects of the nearly 8,000 ft. elevation. Then we lazed around, napped, and bathed in the free showers fed by hot springs. When we were having dinner in the café, John recognized Billy Goat walking by the windows and invited him to join us at our table and visit. Billy Goat was hiking a familiar section of the high country he knew so well. He visited with us briefly, assuring us that the trail was in good shape ahead of us, and then he was on his way. After our meal, John, Jennie and I all enjoyed the lovely setting and the pleasant campground with fir forest and meadows around us.

On the next day we were to find out just how well John and Jennie had acclimated to the altitude in their one day and two nights there. We hiked about 12 miles, climbing about 1,500 ft. to 9,700, and I discovered what good shape I was in at that point by contrast. John said that was his hardest climb ever, and Jennie announced that this would be her last PCT hike. My weeks of hiking, mostly at altitude, gave me a major advantage in acclimating and conditioning.

I was determined we should camp nearby, as I had planned, but we found that the rugged land was on a pretty steep slope. We stopped as dusk approached, and I clambered up above the trail to where we saw a few small trees, hoping to find a level area. That was a good spot, so I left my pack and descended to the trail to get the others. They laboriously made their own way up, Jennie refusing to let me carry her pack. We chose our tent sites, and we had room to spare in the small, park-like setting. Soon I descended again to the trail to tell two young men and a preteen daughter about our level campsite discovery, and they clambered up to join us. Young Samantha was carrying a pretty large pack for the very first time, and she was very cheerful. Her dad was proud of her.

We were hiking along the eastern wall of a deep gorge. The John Muir Trail was separated from the PCT here, the JMT making its way along the western side of the gorge. We could see that the other trail passed beside Shadow Lake. The lake was exquisitely situated in a pocket on the western wall, and John exclaimed that it looked like a fine fishing spot worthy of a separate hike. I agreed, and we hoped to return to it someday.

On Friday we were doing better, hiking downhill and then level awhile. We met Tom again, now hiking south from Tuolumne to Red's Meadow. We also met Billy Goat again, also southbound. I rinsed my laundry at Thousand Island Lake, where we were joined by a man who asked if he could buy fishing gear from us. He said he had hiked there for his two-week vacation, set up camp and then was fishing and exploring at a leisurely pace. A bear habituated to raiding hikers' and fishermen's food at the lake had torn up his pack at his camp, devoured his food, and then searched along the lake shore until it found the man's stringer of caught fish lying in shallow water. The bear devoured the fish also, destroying the man's fishing gear in the process.

Over the Hill

Now with ten days remaining of his vacation, the poor guy was preparing to hike back out and go home. He had been out sightseeing when the bear came, so he watched helplessly from a safe distance. His vacation was ruined. He said he had kept only snacks and cooking oil in his bear proof canister, so now he could not enjoy his vacation with most of his food in the belly of the bear. We had no fishing gear to offer him, as I had left mine at home, and we had little food to spare for him.

We hiked up another 1,000 ft. and over Donahue Pass at 11,056 ft. with no real trouble. John and Jennie did well, much better acclimated now – but we all huffed and puffed a lot. My main regret was that I had left my gloves with Zhita, not expecting the mornings to be so cold. I needed to grip my trekking poles, and my hands hurt in the cold morning air. We arrived at Vogelsang Trail where I had hoped to meet up with Kirsten and our friend Gigi, but they were not there. I asked other hikers if they had seen them, but none had seen the women I described. Disappointed, we headed on toward Tuolumne Meadow.

I was intrigued when we met a southbound hiker carrying a compact backpack. He clearly was not carrying a bear canister in that pack. I understood that a federal law required hikers in Yosemite to keep their food in bear-proof containers at night. We chatted about the trail for a moment and then I asked him how he protected his food in this national park where bears are notorious for getting hiker's food which has merely been hung in a tree at night. He was very pleased to tell us the story of why he carried no canister, despite the clever hungry bears and the law.

The man said he and a friend had been hiking in a remote area in the mountains one time when they came upon a cabin with smoke rising from its chimney. They stopped to visit with the occupant, who turned out to be a woman living alone. When he noticed that she had several ordinary metal garbage cans outside her cabin with easily removable lids, he asked how she kept the bears from ransacking them. She said she hired a man to save his urine and come to her cabin once a week to pour his urine on the ground around the garbage cans. That kept the bears away. She said female urine doesn't work, so she had to hire a man to do it. Our hiker decided then that he did not need to carry a bulky bear canister any more. He would simply pour his urine on the ground around his tent each night and then take his pack with his food into the tent with him.

We exclaimed our astonishment that such a surprising remedy would work. He acknowledged that once he had been stopped by a man who griped that he had tried this touted remedy, but one night a bear had ripped his tent open while the man quaked in terror inside. The bear pulled out his pack with his food, demolished the pack and ate the man's food. Our hiker simply shrugged and said, "There's exceptions to every rule." He continued to rely on his remedy, and he answered my further question negatively – he had not been bothered by a bear nor fined by a Park Ranger. He appeared to be in his fifties, old enough to know what he was doing – but somehow we weren't convinced. He was more daring than we were prepared to be.

Continuing on, we arrived at Tuolumne Meadows in the afternoon to find Kirsten and Gigi at the road together with my friend Gene. All was well. Gigi, who had hiked into the Grand Canyon with us in 2004, now felt she wasn't in condition to hike with Kirsten out to meet us. They simply awaited our arrival and joined in our celebration. Gene was unable to schedule a hike with me this year, but he wanted at least to meet me on the trail. The meadow was a short drive from his cabin in Foresta, a private inholding of cabins within Yosemite boundaries which predated the creation of the park.

Zhita arrived soon after Gene's departure, and the celebrating continued. The highlight of our celebration was dinner at the Ahwanee Lodge. Then Zhita and I went to a motel outside the park while the other four bedded down in a park campground. Next morning Kirsten and Gigi headed for home, and Zhita and I took John and Jennie sightseeing in Yosemite, relishing the gorgeous scenery and the fascinating sight of climbers making their precarious way up the sheer vertical rock face of Half Dome. Then we drove back to retrieve John's truck and all headed for a motel in Mammoth.

Tuesday morning we were up early. Dressed in the clean clothes Zhita brought for me, I refilled my pack with the final week's food and supplies. John and Jennie headed for Phoenix, John strongly regretting once again to be leaving me on the trail. Zhita and I returned to Tuolumne for my final week's trek for the year. After hugs and kisses, she headed for home and I set off on Soda Springs Road.

The Tuolumne River was turbulent and lovely, with waterfalls. It was good to be alone in the woods again, though I enjoyed talking with occasional hikers along the way. On Thursday I camped at 9,500 ft., achieving my old routine of about 15 mile days below 10,000 ft. I met Billy Goat once again, had a brief chat in passing as he was heading south. On Friday there was a helicopter searching the area I was in, and I learned from another hiker that they were searching for a young hiker who did not show up when expected. The next day I talked to a Search and Rescue man who was on the trail looking for the missing hiker. Later I learned that the missing hiker had been found, hobbled by a twisted ankle, and he was safely retrieved.

Sunday I hiked to Lake Harriet then inadvertently got off on a trail to campsites around the lake. On my way back to the PCT I made another mistake and got on an old route of the PCT, now called West Walker River Trail, as I learned when I descended to a trail junction with a sign. I was now heading for Walker Meadow, clearly not in my guidebook. A few more trail signs would have been helpful. It was getting late, and I decided to camp where I was and then make a fresh start in the morning to get back to the PCT.

A Forest Ranger came walking through, and he confirmed that the new trail would return me to the PCT. He made me move my tent, for I had carelessly set it up too close to the trail, where I thought no one would notice. Then he asked where I was heading next. When I told him my wife would be picking me up at Sonora Pass, he asked if I would count the number and approximate diameters of fallen trees on the PCT on my way to the pass and then leave a note for him at the Forest Service office nearby. He was scouting for trail maintenance projects, and I was glad to help him with that.

Next morning I hiked two miles back up to the PCT near a steel bridge. Before me lay another 17 miles to tomorrow's meeting place with Zhita, with a climb of 2,200 ft. The last ten miles ahead of me was alpine hiking above the tree line at 10,640 to 10,830 ft. elevation. I planned to camp one night at altitude, then go on to reach the pass after an easy final section.

A cold wind blew hard when I reached the alpine part, so I wore my fleece pullover, my rain jacket and my knit hat pulled down over my ears and at times my bandana over my mouth and nose. I wished again I had not left my gloves behind to minimize my pack weight, and I was glad John and Jennie were not with me. This was desolate country of wind-scoured rock but with spectacular views of the rugged, craggy mountain ridges. I marveled at seeing occasional small patches of plants with blossoms only an inch or two high, so hardy on this cold barren rock. Then I was amazed to see small bees busily working the blossoms. Of course, these isolated little flowers required pollinators, but I was astonished that any bees could survive in such a cold, desolate environment. I was not tempted to pee for them.

Most of the trail in this section was level or gently sloped, and I was energized by my exposure to the cold wind. Perhaps it would be possible to push on through without stopping to camp until I descended from this frigid height. I would try.

At last I reached where the trail descended toward the pass and lonely paved Highway 108. It was beginning to get dark when I found a level place to camp sheltered from the wind. As I was preparing dinner, a young woman appeared, hiking south. We exchanged greetings, and when I saw that she was continuing up to the long alpine stretch above, I called after her. I warned her about the exposed barren terrain ahead and the strong, cold wind. She was undeterred, and I called out "Good luck!" She had a lot of pluck, and I hoped she was well prepared.

Monday morning I awoke to find that all of my water was frozen solid. My little thermometer still read 40 degrees, the coldest it would register, but there was no mistaking the fact that it was freezing cold. I had a dry breakfast of energy bars and packed up my gear. Soon I reached the road at Sonora Pass. I had hiked 370 miles on the PCT in the fall, plus a few miles inadvertently on other trails. It wasn't all easy, and I was sobered once again to learn about my limitations. Still, I felt very good about my accomplishment for the year.

Zhita showed up soon after. We were both very happy to see each other. I was also glad to get in the warm car and drink a lot of her water. We stopped at a Forest Service Ranger Station to drop off my note reporting that there were 17 downed trees, mostly small, on that last part of the trail. We headed for home.

When we arrived home on Tuesday, our first phone call was from my older daughter Darbi calling from New Mexico to tell me that my stepmother had died. On Thursday Zhita took me to the airport.

2006 Suncups

2006

This year I wanted to see the part of the PCT in the Sierras which I had skipped in 2005. Trail lore I had read said that snow melt in the Sierras typically was accompanied by clouds of mosquitoes in June, so I decided to begin this part of my 2006 hike in July. My main hike for the year would begin in August at Sonora Pass where I had finished hiking in 2005 and would continue past Lake Tahoe and on to start into northern California. I was to learn a lesson this year about the importance of checking the PCTA and other websites for current, detailed information about trail conditions far from my home environment.

July

I decided to hike this Sierra section of the trail from north to south, preferring to make a 3,000 ft. descent at the end rather than start out with such an abrupt ascent. I also wanted to tackle Mt. Whitney near the southern end of this section after hiking for a while at altitude, when I would be better acclimated. After my now usual planning, preparing and training, Zhita and I set out driving the Explorer to Lake Edison on July 8. Again we stayed at Vermillion Lodge for two nights so I could begin to get acclimated to the altitude and Zhita could start the hazardous drive home refreshed.

The pine forest around the lake still held some snow and some soft, mushy ground, discouraging us from exploring very far on our free day together. At the lodge I learned that the previous winter's snowpack in the Sierras had been twice its usual depth, though at the lake's altitude of 7,800 ft. the snow and mud just looked messy now. In a bare patch of dirt among the trees we found a few small red snow plants, a rare treat I had never seen. This plant has no chlorophyll, and it gets its nourishment from fungi which grow underground in a symbiotic relationship with tree roots. The snow plant is native only to mountains in the western US, where its small stalks of bright red flowers appear in the spring.

I began hiking south from the lake on Monday, July 10. As I began gaining altitude, I found that the snow was indeed deeper than when I was in the Sierras in August of the previous year. It was harder hiking in the snow, and it became challenging at higher elevations. Still, I hiked over Selden Pass at 10,900 ft., simply stopping often to catch my breath. It was slow going, but I found it reassuring that it was no harder than usual for me to get enough oxygen at the higher elevation on the pass. After descending to a lower elevation I called Zhita on the sat phone Thursday morning, feeling more confident. I told her that I was behind schedule, but I was doing okay. She was relieved, as she had sensed from my voice the previous day that I was unsure about my ability to make this hike in the snow.

After my experiences the previous year with puzzling trail junctions, I had done some reading about navigating in the wilderness. I was intrigued to imagine grid lines of longitude and latitude as a transparent conceptual overlay superimposed on the trail. The overlay introduces straight lines not seen in nature, and we use them to help us navigate courses and locate places on our irregular trails in the natural world. Now I was glad to have maps and compass and the guidebook descriptions of the trail, because it wasn't easy to determine the course. Where there were trees, some were marked with reassuring blazes, and sometimes I could see depressions in the snow where earlier hikers had trekked and more recent snow had not fully obliterated the old footprints. But often I depended on my navigation aids and sometimes a bit of guesswork. There were no fresh footprints in the snow.

The PCT route through the Sierras permits hikers to choose a season to hike when their boots usually can strike the ground. I knew that most hikers do that, contending only with patches of snow and ice and occasional snow fields. Hiking in deeper snow and ice was a different enterprise calling for different preparations and training. I also had read that a few hikers use skis or snowshoes to trek the PCT in the Sierras. Many more carry crampons and ice axe and work on skills and conditioning for kicking steps in crusty snow. I had done a little skiing many years ago, and once I had hiked wearing snowshoes. But now, like almost all the hikers I had met, I was neither equipped nor conditioned by training for the challenge of hiking a major distance in snow. (I later read that because of the deep snow this year, most thru hikers either turned back from the Sierras or skipped over them entirely, planning to hike here late in the season or another year.)

What I found at higher elevations was discouraging. On the day I reached Wanda Lake (11,400 ft.) on the alpine slopes approaching Muir Pass (11,955 ft.), I was walking on suncups on the hard, crusty surface of the snow. The deeply dimpled snow looked as if a giant ice cream scoop had been used on it. Though the air was cold, the sun pierced the thin air and began softening the thick crust during the day. Each night the crust froze hard again, only to begin softening once more the following day. The scalloped crust had a slippery surface due to ice in the morning or slush in the afternoon, so I had to walk carefully – and slowly. At times I broke through the crust, postholing into the snow up to my thigh. Each time I had to work to clamber back on top of the snow's crust, balancing my pack and sometimes breaking through again. A few times I plunged into a hidden stream of snowmelt which filled my boot. Then I had to get the boot off my numb foot to empty the water and wring out my sock.

At Wanda Lake I found some rocks and dirt which had warmed enough in the sun to melt a clearing in the snow, so I stopped a bit early in the day to make camp. The trail ahead of me climbing up to Muir Pass was completely blanketed in scalloped, crusty snow. I wondered if anyone had ever before camped on the trail here beside Wanda Lake, where it seemed such a barren, uninviting place to stay. Not bothering to put up my tent, I took advantage of the wind that kept the mosquitoes away.

I had seen no other hikers trying to get through this snow since leaving Lake Edison and no fresh boot prints. I was alone. The absence of any other hikers on this popular trail seemed ominous. I realized now that I needed to research specific local trail conditions and weather before I planned to hike on a section of trail so far from my familiar home environment.

After dinner I reconsidered my hike plan. I discovered that I was averaging only five miles a day on the days I hiked on crusty suncups, now realizing more clearly what had slowed me so over Selden Pass. I could not expect to find any major improvement in trail conditions ahead. The mountains before me carried a heavy snowpack as far as I could see, and there were five passes to cross at about 12,000 ft. I had hiked about 40 miles from Lake Edison, and I still had 50 miles to go to reach Zhita in Onion Valley. I would come to no roads before I reached her. How many miles of trail before me would be crusted with suncups?

Five miles per day! I couldn't carry enough food to hike from Lake Edison to Onion Valley at this rate – and I certainly didn't have enough food with me now to hike 50 miles farther at my uncertain pace. I was very disappointed. I felt okay, I was acclimated to the altitude, the mountains were beautiful – and I really wanted to finish this section of the trail. It was tempting to keep going and try to tough it out, but I knew that getting hungry would not be the only consequence. I needed more fuel for my muscles to be able to continue like this. With no other hikers currently in this section of the trail, continuing now would mean increasing isolation. It would be foolhardy to continue, but I could hardly bear to bail out of the Sierras again. Defeated by suncups!

I was very thankful for the many details in the guidebook about side trails leading out from the PCT, for now I had an unanticipated need for information about finding a way off the trail to a passable road. There were frustratingly few trail signs in this unfamiliar terrain, so I was very dependent on the guidebook for finding my way out. The guidebook said there was a trail to Florence Lake, and the lake was at a lower elevation where I expected to find much less snow. Zhita and I had driven near it on our way to Edison Lake.

Very reluctantly I called Zhita Saturday morning to tell her I was turning back. Once again I was very glad to have the sat phone. I asked her to come to Florence Lake to pick me up, driving that crazy road again almost as far as going back to Edison Lake. I told her I could get there the next day.

When I called on Sunday to tell her that I could not reach Florence Lake until the next day, Zhita and her granddaughter were already well on their way to meet me. I was still moving slowly in more snow than I expected. Zhita said they would find a motel in Fresno with a swimming pool where they could find relief from the relentless heat. I would have like to share some of that heat in the snowy Sierras!

When I reached Florence Lake (with only scattered snow at the lower elevation of 7,200 ft.), I saw a rattlesnake more than three feet long. It disappeared under a bush beside the trail near the boat dock, and I assumed it had gone into a hole. I called on the phone at the dock to ask for a ride, and the launch showed up on schedule at midday. When I arrived at the other shore I went in to the store to buy snacks, and I told the proprietress about the snake. She was concerned, because some children would be going there soon for a short hike. Reluctantly, she decided that she needed to kill the snake. I agreed to ride with her on the next launch back and show her where I had seen it. She put a shovel, a rake and a hoe by the door to take with her. However, Zhita arrived at the store soon after, and the proprietress quietly left for the next scheduled launch trip while I was greeting my wife and granddaughter.

Zhita's Story 2006

By 2006, as our learning continued, Jim and I thought we knew how to handle our meet-ups. I knew there would be adventures as we planned to meet in places that neither of us had ever seen, places without sign-posts, or even people to ask for help, but I was starting to get used to this aspect of our adventure—and I was well aware that good anecdotes would pop up like wildflowers on the trail—or like lightning strikes in the wilderness. It wasn't long before we had the first "lightning strike"....

This year there was one other very special factor that would become a part of our first meet-up. My daughter and son-in-law were going to India on a mission, and my 6-year-old granddaughter, Zhita Lynne, (whom I refer to as ZZ, the nickname that my family used for me when I was growing up) would be staying with me. I loved the idea of having time with ZZ all to myself and I knew that Grandpa would enjoy seeing her at our first trail meet-up. We were ready for our adventure.... But I didn't imagine that complications would start so soon when Jim discovered the "sun cups" in the Sierra snow. Five days after I had delivered him to the trail, he called to say that he had to bail out and that I should plan to meet him on the following day. Z and I had to get ready....

I hastily packed the car with essentials for ZZ, including books, crafts, games and snacks. She and I climbed into the Explorer, and headed on our way—and then the "Check Engine" light came on. What did that mean? What should I do? With ZZ in the car, I could not take risks; so I turned back home and talked to our young neighbor David to ask for his help. He and I checked the Explorer manual and David decided that I could probably continue safely. So ZZ and I were on the road again. However, this time when the engine light came on with warning of a potential engine fire, I pulled off the freeway and returned home. This time I asked David if I could borrow his car—in exchange for his use of our new Prius. He was very happy to make the exchange.

ZZ and I were on the road yet again.... Up over the hill and past the Grapevine, a Southern California traveler's landmark, the long, steep descent from Tejon Pass down into the desert near Bakersfield on Interstate 5. I stopped to get ZZ something for lunch. Fortunately,

I checked my cell phone; the message from Jim said that he had miscalculated the meet-up time and he would not be able to meet us till the next day....

What should we do? Returning to LA seemed like a poor option. We had gotten this far so we would keep going, stay in a motel in Fresno and continue on the following day. Have you ever been to Fresno in the middle of July? It was a hellishly hot place of refuge—but it was a place of refuge. We checked into a motel that had air conditioning and a swimming pool, and we enjoyed both. ZZ was a bit disappointed that I wouldn't let her get into the pool until the beastly hot sun began to wane and provided some shade. But she was delighted to jump in eventually.

The next day was a joy as we actually found Jim at Florence Lake, drove back to Fresno to spend another night, and started home the next morning. Back in LA, we took the Explorer to the shop; and ZZ gave both of us the most welcome hugs. Life is good....

Jim

It was wonderful to see the two Zhitas, and they were relieved to find me well and in good spirits. After stashing my gear in the back of the borrowed car, I discovered that the launch had left without me. So I took the wheel of the car and we set out for Fresno for a night at the motel. Next morning we drove on to LA.

August

My main hike for 2006 began with my friend Gene. On Friday, August 4, Gene picked me up and we drove to Dardanelles in the Sonora Pass area in northern California. After a night in a nearby motel, we drove to the pass. I had suggested to Gene that this year we hike together for three miles from Sonora Pass at 9,600 ft. to a saddle on the Sierra crest, at 10,500 ft. the highest point on the PCT north of Sonora Pass.

The guidebook cautioned that this high country might have heavy snow and ice even through late July, especially on the north slopes of mountains. After my recent experience with sun cups on this year's lingering snowpack in the Sierras, I searched online for current trail information before we left. I was relieved to tell Gene there were no recent reports of impassable sections of trail. We should be able to walk through what snow remained.

When Gene's friends Kim and her husband Kevin learned that Gene was planning to hike with me in this remote high country, they decided to join us. Early in the year, Gene, Kim, Darbi and I had backpacked together into Havasupai Canyon. Now this day hike would be a lark. Kim and Kevin drove through the night to get from LA to the pass that Saturday morning, taking turns driving and sleeping. I noted again what a luxury it is for me to be retired, not bound by work schedules.

Each of us greatly enjoyed hiking together in the spectacular landscape high in the Sierras. We walked at times through manageable patches of softening snow on the trail which had been cut into the steep mountain slopes as we gradually climbed to the saddle. Where pines adorned the weathered granite, they were stunted by cold winter winds. Finally, above the tree line at the saddle, we stopped for a break. Looking north, we could see a series of mountains and ridges continuing for many miles into the distance. I was reminded of a line from Robert Frost, "And miles to go before I sleep." (When I related this incident to Zhita, she was reminded of the beginning of that line, "But I have promises to keep..." Needing to hike those miles must be compatible with needing to return home safely.)

My companions turned back at the saddle. Kevin had to get back to Los Angeles that same day so he could present his half hour radio talk show at 5:30 the next morning. Gene would drive to his cabin in Yosemite, then return home the following day. I could hardly believe my good fortune in having such friends with whom to share some time on the PCT adventure. They certainly went far out of their way to join me this time! I wished them safe travel home and then continued my quest.

Much as I enjoyed hiking with my friends, I now welcomed the quiet solitude as I continued climbing and descending the rugged ridges alone. I was still determined to return again and hike the rest of the trail in the Sierras. I had begun hiking as a healthy recreation in retirement, and for me it had developed into a challenging adventure. An oldtimer with limited experience, I had set out to hike a trail far longer than any I had ever imagined trying to hike. I was succeeding, one section at a time. I wanted to see it all.

My thoughts wandered while hiking alone, and I occasionally reminisced about experiences in my past. In high school I could never decide whether I wanted to work with my hands or my mouth. Doctor, lawyer, engineer, teacher – I thought many careers sounded attractive. I joined the Navy to get the GI Bill to finance going to college, and I became an electronic technician, repairing ship's radars. I worked in a shipyard for a year after my Navy experience while I continued to sort through career options. Active in a Presbyterian church then, I settled on studying philosophy in preparation for the ministry. My girlfriend shared my vision, and we married and set out on this career path together. I enrolled in San Diego State College. But in a few years religion lost its appeal for me, replaced by my enthusiasm for more academic philosophy. The transition to the new career plan was difficult for me and for my wife.

I had gone on to study philosophy as a graduate student at UCLA, earning an MA and a C. Phil. (Candidate in Philosophy degree, having been advanced to candidacy for the PhD). But I had begun teaching well before I completed my student work, in order to support my growing family. A couple of years later, during a prolonged period of personal turmoil, I divorced my wife and struggled with my responsibilities for teaching fulltime and writing my dissertation, all while making a new start in life as an unmarried man and an absentee father. After I had about 50 pages of dissertation accepted, I decided it was all wrong and I had to start over. My dissertation advisor protested strenuously, urging me to finish and get my degree. My dissertation so far was good enough.

He said I could write an article later and refute myself if I wanted to revise my account. To no avail. I struggled to rewrite.

Finally, at the end of eight years of teaching philosophy, mostly at Northern Arizona University, I completed my last teaching job as a one-year sabbatical replacement at Texas Tech. Totally frustrated with writing my dissertation, I gave up my career and turned away from my friends and my way of life. I very reluctantly resigned myself to never finishing my dissertation, so I no longer saw a future for myself in teaching. A fan of the poetry of Ezra Pound when I was at NAU, I liked to quote his verse,

> *O God, O Venus, O Mercury, patron of thieves,*
> *Lend me a little tobacco-shop,*
> > *Or install me in any profession*
> *Save this damn'd profession of writing,*
> > *Where one needs one's brains all the time.*

My girlfriend at the time had enshrined the poem in a painting for me.

I had returned from Texas to California, where I went back to doing shipyard work as an electrician. I thought my hands would never again be clean. I struggled with the transition from a professional in a classroom to an electrician in the bowels of a ship. Where I had formerly enjoyed taking responsibility for teaching my classes, now I needed to relearn a trade from the younger men I toiled with. I worked harder than most everyone, determined to keep my job as I learned.

Sometimes at the end of the day, I admired the motorcycles several of the men rode to work, and I decided to get one for myself. When I asked for advice about the kind of bike to get, they recommended a 350cc engine, not too heavy or too powerful. I began looking at ads. My brother soon called from his home in Phoenix to tell me about an ad in his newspaper, offering to sell a used Kawasaki 350 at a bargain price. He had called the seller and was assured that the bike was in running condition. I quickly read the California driver's manual for motorcyclists and took a written test to get a learner's permit. I bought a helmet, and I got a ride to Phoenix with my former girlfriend and another friend. John took me to look at the bike. After the owner showed me how to operate the controls, I rode it around the block – my first try at operating a motorcycle. I bought the bike, and my brother and I got it into his pickup. Then on the street in front of John's house I practiced for a little while, learning to coordinate using the clutch and shifting gears and applying gas or brakes.

Next morning, soon after rush hour, I made an exciting trip across town in Phoenix traffic, once stalling in the middle of an intersection while fumbling with the gearshift, clutch and gas. I finally reached the freeway (not legal with a learner's permit) and headed for home. By the time I reached Blythe at the California border, the bike engine was sputtering. I found a mechanic in Ehrenberg who replaced the sparkplugs and tuned up the little engine. I slept on the beach beside the Colorado River that night, having brought my sleeping bag and a change of clothes.

On the California freeway the next day I got bored with sitting on the bike at a monotonous steady speed, so I decided to get off the freeway at Banning for a side trip on what I knew to be a winding road up Mt. San Jacinto toward Idylwild. At last I experienced a taste of what I had imagined riding a motorcycle could be like. Then I returned to the freeway and rode on to my home in Long Beach, uneventfully. I knew I had been rash and very lucky, but I had really enjoyed the weekend adventure as a distraction from frustration and disappointment. Next morning I rode my bike to work, now "one of the guys." I would adapt to this new life. (The bike ran for only a year, during which I scared myself a few times but never spilled it.)

Life went on. With another girlfriend, I married again, divorced again. I worked my way up to foreman electrician. Later I met and then finally married Zhita, the best decision of my life, at last. My third marriage was wonderfully successful, and partnering with Zhita for many years enabled me to live a good life. Later I started a wholesale electric supply business, and after six years I sold it to a regional chain whose owner had deeper pockets and vastly more experience. Finally I retired as the manager of what had been my shop.

Like other old men, I have my ample share of mistakes, regrets and failures as well as joys and achievements. I cannot complain overall. Still, having failed to complete my dissertation sometimes haunted me. Now the prospect of completing a very different but still a major, self-chosen goal offered the prospect of closure to offset the memory of that unfinished dissertation. I needed to hike the entire PCT. The remaining 50 miles in the High Sierras was important. I would hike it yet.

Returning to the present, on Thursday, August 10, I reached Highway 50, where Zhita was to meet me. I had hiked about 75 miles. She drove up from LA and arrived shortly after I did. By this time we had decided on a routine which Zhita had urged of my taking two nights and a full day off each week to resupply. That gave me more time to rest, take hot showers, eat restaurant meals, and sleep in a real bed. Many younger hikers would scoff at taking such frequent days off, but at age 70, it made a welcome difference for me. Having Zhita as my support team and my partner clearly was my great good fortune. For this resupply break we went to South Lake Tahoe, just a few miles away, then returned to the trail on Saturday.

The convenience of having South Lake Tahoe so near the PCT proved to be a mixed blessing. Hiking north once more, I entered Desolation Wilderness, so named because the glaciers that once scoured out the many lake basins had removed most of the soil, leaving little to support trees. The trail through the open, rugged terrain offers many beautiful views of lakes among the mountains as well as convenient water sources for hikers. Much of the PCT in this section coincides with the Tahoe-Yosemite Trail and also with a portion of the Tahoe Rim Trail. The combination of convenient location and beauty leads to what the PCT guidebook says is the greatest density of hikers per square mile of any roadless area in California. Desolation Wilderness is popular, and solitude is here replaced by friendly social activity.

I continued hiking north, past Interstate 80 near storied Donner Pass and on to Highway 49 near Sierra City. Zhita found me waiting beside the highway when she arrived on Friday, August 18. I had hiked 105 miles. She remarked that I looked exhausted and deliriously happy. We toured a fascinating mining museum on my day off the next day, indulging my interest in the now-shelved plan to build a model railroad layout based in part on my paternal grandfather's brief employment loading coal onto trains.

On Sunday morning I set out from the highway in fine sunny weather. The trail followed a switchback course up the steep slope. Soon, noticing a loose rock on the trail which seemed a possible hazard for horses, I kicked it aside. My maneuver revealed a small hole that went straight down into the dirt, and bees came streaming out of it in furious defense. I was assaulted as I struggled to run uphill with my freshly loaded pack. When I stopped to frantically pull my head net out of my pack and pull it over my head, I was repeatedly stung on my hands and through my shirt. Mercifully the trail soon ascended more gradually above the highway, and in a few more minutes I was able to get far enough away that the creatures left me. I shuddered to imagine a horse and rider having disturbed that rock.

After climbing just two more switchbacks I met a southbound solo hiker whom I warned about the nest. He was very grateful for the warning, because he was allergic to bee stings. A single sting could cause anaphylaxis, a severe and potentially fatal reaction. He was carrying epinephrine to counteract that, but he couldn't be certain he could self-administer it in time if he were stung. He said my warning might have saved his life. For once I thought it was fully justified for someone to take a shortcut off the trail past a few switchbacks as he made his way around the dangerous nest and down to the road. I was sobered by the discovery that some hikers brave hazards the rest of us never imagine.

It was pretty warm hiking uphill with a full pack, so I was glad to remove the head net when I was sure I was no longer perceived as a threat. The breeze on my face was welcome. After less than an hour on the trail, I certainly was alert to the hazards of the wilderness. Now I was particularly glad I kept my head net in an outside pocket of my pack. I had stowed it there for quick retrieval, in case of mosquitoes.

Two days later, when I was ready to take a break at midday, I saw an inviting tree stump at a convenient height for a seat about 30 ft. from the trail, and it was in the shade. I waded through the green undergrowth and happily removed my pack. I sat down and took off my hat and my boots and looked around. As I was reaching for my lunch I realized that something was buzzing around me insistently. Suddenly I felt a sting; I was being attacked again! I jammed my feet in my boots, slapped my hat on, snatched out my head net and donned it, hastily shrugged my pack on, grabbed my poles and ran, sort of. Luckily, this time I did not have to go far to get out of the bees' perceived territory. I continued walking a little farther until I found a suitable log to sit on which was close to the trail. Here I was not disturbed. I was relieved that in my haste to leave the previous stump I had somehow managed to grab everything I needed; I had only a few more stings. Now when I cautiously removed my boots again, I found a smashed bee in the bottom of one. I had never before been stung so many times in one week. I remained on the alert, for I now remembered reading that too many stings within a short time can cause anaphylaxis even in someone not previously allergic to bee stings.

Four days later I arrived at Highway 70 at the Belden Town Bridge, having hiked 92 miles. Zhita picked me up and we drove down to Oroville where we stayed with my cousin Chuck and his wife Bev. Chuck, a retired exterminator, listened to my story about my encounter with the bees. Hearing that I saw one insect sting my hand repeatedly, he corrected my story, explaining that I had been stung by yellow jackets rather than bees. Bees leave their stingers behind when they sting, so they can't attack again.

Soon it was back to the trail one more time to hike my last part for the year. On Wednesday I stopped to take a picture of the official halfway marker on the trail, announcing that it was 1,325 miles from Mexico and from Canada. The sign did not express the exuberance of the unofficial painted rock I had passed a couple of miles before which claimed to mark the halfway point, but I was pleased to see the official sign. My own hike was short of halfway, due to the skipped piece in the Sierras, but I was well on my way.

On Thursday, August 31 Zhita and I met at Highway 36 west of Lake Almanor, and she drove me back to my cousin's. I had hiked about 416 miles since Sonora Pass. It was a pretty good hike for the year in spite of the yellow jackets and in spite of my having bailed out after only 40 miles on the PCT on sun cups in the Sierras. I was determined that I would return to those mountains. I needed to hike the whole trail.

We celebrated my hike for the year with Chuck and Bev. Next day we drove home.

2007 Natural Beauty

Some people never see a sunrise, or if they see it, never thought nothing about it. I think every sun that rises done it just for me.

WYATT MOORE
CADDO LAKE ORAL HISTORY PROJECT OF
EAST TEXAS STATE UNIVERSITY

The Pacific Crest Trail makes a long traverse of the length of California. From the southern border with Mexico to the northern border with Oregon, the trail follows mountain crests where possible through an astonishing variety of terrain. From arid desert lowlands through semi-arid lands and on into mountains at altitudes which command yields of moisture from passing storms, the trail presents a rich tapestry of environments. I had hiked about 1350 miles through the state to see three quarters of what the trail here offers its travelers. For this year's hike I planned to trek through Lassen Volcanic National Park and more mountains, forests and wilderness areas on my way toward the Oregon border.

Zhita and I drove to San Francisco on Friday, August 10 to stay at Wendy and Greg's while they were away on a mission in Nicaragua. On Saturday we drove to Red Bluff to get my wilderness permit and buy a jug of water, then on to Hat Creek Mesa which the guidebook described as the site of a hot, dry stretch of trail. We found a place to cache the water and then returned to Red Bluff for the night.

I had rented a Global Star satellite phone this year at a bargain rate, due to the failure of some of their satellites. My friend Gene, an engineer and a consultant for a satellite manufacturer, had explained to me that Global Star was in trouble, as their satellites were failing prematurely and the cost of replacement was prohibitive. I was warned that the phone would be less reliable that year, and that is one forecast that proved to be very accurate. I often gave up trying to get a signal, so I failed to call Zhita more often than not. Some bargain. An emergency call would be unlikely to succeed.

On Sunday morning I began my hike where I left off in 2006 at Highway 36 near Lake Almanor. It was a sunny day in the pine forest, though the trail proceeded to cross several roads and logged areas along the way. The trail led into Lassen Park, and in addition to old, cold lava I saw the lingering volcanic activity which is an attraction of the park. Boiling Springs Lake lived up to its name, with fumaroles and stinky mudpots. It provided an interesting contrast to the forested terrain I most enjoyed along the PCT.

The lava was sometimes very rough, with wide crevices between large, jumbled boulders with sharply jagged surfaces which discouraged any attempt to walk or jump on them. Trail construction appeared heroic across such rough lava where it extended in long, wide fields covering the steep mountain slopes. It appeared that many hours must have been spent bringing wheelbarrow loads of smaller pieces of lava to fill the crevices between boulders to create a surface for the trail across, finished off with more wheelbarrow loads of dirt and lava grit to make it walkable. I noted that tracks on the trail showed that deer and other wildlife used the convenient PCT to cross the lava fields.

One evening as I stretched out in my tent for the night among the pine trees, I was startled to hear rustling noises nearby. I listened intently, trying to figure out what creature could be making so much noise close to my tent. My food was hanging from a low tree branch this time, safeguarded only against hungry mice, rats or squirrels. Now I thought it sounded as if an unexpected bear might be helping itself to my food. Would the backpack in my tent smell appetizing? Would I? My heart in my throat, I opened a tent zipper enough to let me peer out with my headlamp to look for the intruder. It was a deer. The bold animal, only ten yards away, calmly looked up at my light and then continued browsing noisily in the bushes.

Sheepishly, I thought about all the times I had been alarmed by sounds outside my tent at night. Usually I quickly realized that some small creature was rustling about in the leaves or needle duff on the ground, sometimes in the bushes. I needed to be alert to danger if it threatened, but I rarely lost sleep over it. However, once I had had to take a little more trouble to accommodate a wild creature.

On another night, as I was snuggling down into my sleeping bag, I felt movement underneath me. Startled, I felt around in the darkness with my hand, trying to figure out what was happening. I found that the movement was confined to a small spot under my sleeping bag. Something was determinedly pushing up against the tent floor and my hand. There was no sound. Finally it dawned on me. I had erected my tent on the edge of a small meadow, avoiding the mounds of dirt marking entrances to tunnels which I supposed were dug by gophers. But I'd placed my tent where it covered one small hole unmarked by such a mound, thinking it must be an old abandoned hole. Now the hole's occupant was insistently trying to get out. Would it chew a hole into my tent? Grudgingly, while laughing at myself for my blunder, I got out of my bag and out of my tent. Dressed only in my briefs in the chilly darkness, I emptied my tent and took it down, moving it to a spot nearby which I made sure was free of holes into the underground. I set up my tent again and moved my gear and myself back inside. Hereafter I would be more careful when I looked for a tent site in the vicinity of gopher holes.

Zipped inside my tent I was pretty safe from pests such as mosquitoes, scorpions, and snakes. Simply ensuring that no food or food wrappers were in my tent at night made it unlikely that mice or rats would chew a hole in the tent in order to get inside. Bears, lions and other predators were also unlikely to try to get into the tent if they did not smell food inside, assuming they were not so hungry that my own smell enticed them. A hiker deals with nature on nature's terms, far from our routine expectations in civilization. We accommodate.

Some wildlife encounters were a simple delight, watching creatures in their natural setting without disturbing them. A particularly memorable experience happened one morning when I took a break, clambering a few feet above the trail cut into a mountain slope. Pine trees were scattered among the grasses where I sat, and when I was still, it was very quiet. Before I dug into my pack for a snack, I was startled to see a small animal approaching on the trail below me. Without making a sound, a red fox trotted toward me. I did not move. The fox was unaware of my presence above the trail, and it padded along below me and continued out of sight. The red fur on that fox was beautiful! I had never seen a fox in the wild, and I learned later that these Sierra Red Foxes are so rare that I'm unlikely ever to see another. I read that less than 50 of those animals are likely to be alive today. Having seen the luxuriant red fur so close by, I could well understand why trappers and hunters had pursued them so devastatingly before they were protected as an endangered species. I would love to have such an animal to pet, caressing that gorgeous fur!

When hiking on the PCT was new to me, I was keenly alert to the responsibilities of making appropriate choices about all the details of daily life in the wild. Managing my water supply, eating and drinking enough, often enough, watching where I stepped and keeping track of roughly where I was, staying on the right trail, choosing suitable places and times to make camp, finding adequate and timely locations for toileting in the wilderness, even simply deciding when to get up in the morning and prepare to start hiking and then doing it promptly, all called for my attention. Especially when I was hiking alone, these novel and important responsibilities frequently kept me focused. But gradually I realized that, no longer such a novice, I was taking these increasingly routine responsibilities in stride. Easily distracted by my enjoyment of the rich variety of scenery around me and sometimes by my discomforts, I now had to learn to be careful not to neglect those formerly riveting responsibilities.

Case in point: As I was hiking late one morning I discovered that my camera was missing from its place on my pack belt. My camera case must have slipped off when I removed my pack at a rest stop that day, so there were only a few likely places to look. Surely I would have noticed if the camera case had been missing when I first loaded up in the morning. Chagrined at having lost my camera with its many photos and my only means of taking more, I needed to go back to search for it. A search was a very unwelcome interruption, but it was important to try.

For the rest of the morning and into the afternoon I retraced my steps until I found my camera lying beside a creek where I had filtered water and rested earlier that day. I tied the camera case to my pack belt buckle with a spare boot lace so it could not slide off the belt again and then began retracing my steps. I lost most of a day recovering the camera – what a waste! Now at the end of the day I would be near the community of Old Station, where the Heitmans were resident trail angels who invited hikers to spend a night on their lawn. I was glad I remembered reading about them online when I was planning this year's hike.

At the Old Station country store I first called Zhita on the pay phone. A working connection, at last. I told her about my lost day, and I described how to find the Crystal Lake Trout Hatchery near Cassel instead of meeting me at Burney Falls as planned. Then I found the Heitmans' phone number on a note to hikers pinned near the phone, and I called them to ask for a ride. Larry was dispatched to pick me up, and he soon arrived at the store. He was the husband and resupply team of Joanne, a section hiker I had met on the trail earlier in the day. We talked about his alternating roles with his wife, taking turns hiking and resupplying. When we reached the Heitmans' home I found Joanne and a couple of other hikers, and Georgi Heitman served us a generous spaghetti dinner. That night I slept in one of the Heitmans' tents already set up in their yard.

Next morning I wanted to get an early start rather than wait for breakfast to be served, so Georgi gave me a warm muffin with marmalade and drove me back to the trail. I really appreciated her generous hospitality. Fortunately I was able to make up some of my lost time by Friday when Zhita returned from San Francisco and waited for me at the fish hatchery. I did not make it by 5:00 as planned, but she was relieved when Joanne and another hiker appeared soon after and asked her if she was Jim's wife. Assured by them that I was okay, Zhita waited until I arrived at 6:30. I had hiked about 76 miles from my starting point, not counting the miles I retraced while retrieving the camera.

Zhita's Story 2007

This year Jim and I have gotten things down to a sort of routine. I know what my responsibilities are, and he knows a lot more about what he is about to face and how he must plan for that. But there is always the unexpected; and this year is no exception.

Once again Jim is carrying a satellite phone; however, this year he has decided to rent from a bargain company. We are to be reminded that the old adage, "You get what you pay for," is stubbornly and woefully true. Sometimes the phone works; sometimes it doesn't…. and, of course, when it doesn't, this adds stress for each of us.

We begin the journey by driving to San Francisco and then on to Red Bluff where we purchase water for Jim's water caching. Seems remarkable to me that you can hide water in a place no more distinct than near-this-tree-and-that-rock, come back in several weeks and expect to find it and for it to be still drinkable; but it works. I'm learning.

This time, we also decide to search for the place where I am to meet Jim at the trail. What a relief to be together as we identify the location—not easily found but at least we have both seen it once. And Jim makes appropriate changes to my map as a guide for me to find it on my own.

The following day is beautiful. I drive Jim to the trail and then leave for San Francisco where I will be staying with daughter Wendy and family for a few days. Unfortunately, Wendy is ill, but it is still an opportunity for me to visit with her and Greg and my dear granddaughter ZZ. And for this first week, I again return to LA. It is a happy moment when, within a few minutes of my arrival home, the phone rings and it is Jim, sounding great and confirming that he is on schedule.

During the following week that I am home alone, I am very busy involved with all the projects that are important in my life. One of my major projects is a youth outreach program that I had developed for the League of Women Voters of Los Angeles. It is my way of pursuing my passion and commitment to promoting an informed and engaged electorate. While most League members tend to be in their fifties and beyond, my concern is that we pass this commitment on to youth. This summer I am working on the plans for our annual Running and Winning Forum, an event at which high school students sit in small round-table discussion groups with people who have held elective office to learn what it means to decide to run for office, plan a political campaign, focus on issues that are important to your community, etc. The event, which is held in the impressive Bradley Tower at the top of LA's City Hall, is an important happening for all participants. Making it happen takes a great deal of time, energy, creativity and angst. As chair of the committee, I feel a huge responsibility—and, of course, the accompanying anxiety and misery. For me, bouts of anxiety and depression are ongoing miseries in my life, and this year is no exception. But the miseries are always bounded by the joys—and collaborating with Jim on his PCT mission is one of the joys—and also, of course, filled with responsibility. ☺

Jim

We stayed in Burney that night to resupply, a very pleasant town. On my day off we visited spectacular Burney Falls together and explored the nature trail. On Sunday, before she headed for home I had Zhita drop me off at Burney Falls, skipping the twelve mile piece of trail from the hatchery to the falls so I could get back on my schedule. I would have liked to hike the skipped piece of trail, but I knew that was unlikely to happen for such a short piece so far from home. The guidebook description of numerous roads crossing the trail there and some private land on which the forest had been clearcut was uninspiring. It was one of the many pieces of the trail still needing protection.

Leaving the falls, I made my way among volcanic ridges and ravines which were often clothed in fir, pine and cedar. When the trail led me among oak trees, I sometimes wore my headnet to fend off pesky little flies which were maddeningly determined to explore my eyes, ears, mouth and nostrils in pursuit of moisture. The flies among the oaks were at least as annoying as the mosquitos were in other areas where the trail passed lakes and streams.

I reached Castle Crags on Friday where I met Gene and his wife Claire at Interstate 5. They gave Zhita a break this week by driving up to meet me for my resupply. Gene was going to hike with me after my day off. They had brought their small dogs, Summer and Pam, and my resupply bag. We went to a motel in Shasta City which they had found online to be dog friendly. Our rooms opened onto a small yard where Summer and Pam could run about. We enjoyed a fine dinner at a nearby restaurant which Gene and Claire knew about. On Saturday we went sightseeing around Mt. Shasta after I had repacked with my fresh clothing and food.

Back at Castle Crags on Sunday morning Gene and I set out on the trail, with Gene carrying a day pack. The trail through the park was routed on lower, more accessible terrain, with views of the granite crags towering above us. We hiked together about eight miles, then we left the PCT briefly on the Dog Trail down to a gravel pit parking area beside a Forest Service road. Claire was there waiting for us with Summer and Pam. Kudos once again to the guidebook for making such planning possible. After our farewells Gene and Claire and the dogs watched as I hiked back up the Dog Trail to return to the PCT.

I hiked on into the Klamath Mountains, where the guidebook said to watch for carnivorous California pitcher plants in marshy areas. In the occasional wet patches I found lots of the lush green cobra-shaped plants, together with the ultramafic rocks on which this variety of plant depends. This type of rock is pale brown because it contains a lot of iron which leaches out in the presence of water. The iron rusts on the surface of the rock. When the rock is freshly broken, as I saw where a horse apparently had kicked off pieces of rock, the dark gray color of the interior of the rock is revealed.

Late on Monday, after climbing 2,000 ft. to a modest 6,500 ft., I looked down on Upper Gumboot Lake a little below the trail. After 14 miles of hiking that day, I was very glad to see the emerald green water and my planned campsite not far from the trail.

Musing at times along the trail, I was often intrigued by the beauty we see in bodies of water. Lakes and rivers, streams and waterfalls all have what strikes me as a compelling appeal in their setting among forests and mountains. We are attracted by the beauty in the sight and sound of the precious liquid so essential to sustain life. It seems to me that water is not just another feature in beautiful landscapes; water is more like a gemstone, standing out and commanding our attention in artful settings. My appreciation was enhanced by being thirsty and highly motivated to get water each day while hiking, of course, but I imagine that this beauty has compelling appeal to people in all cultures and parts of the world, thirsty or not.

In this I think we benefit from countless generations of natural selection. Because of that, it is now in our very nature to be drawn to this loveliness we see in water. It is indeed *attractive*. Needing water, we benefit from this trait in our nature, and natural selection explains our attraction today. How differently we would perceive water if it were corrosive rather than life sustaining! I imagine that in such a different world we might still admire a beautiful landscape with water features, but we would not find the water itself attractive as we do in the real world.

Some of our daughters say that what we benefit from in this case is benevolent design rather than natural selection, achieving the same end. God made us to be attracted to life-sustaining water. I suppose that natural selection then could be part of that design. I think of this view as a conceptual overlay, analogous to the grid lines of longitude and latitude which help to guide travelers navigating a route. A Christian overlay provides direction and meaning in believers' lives. A religious perspective of the world we live in can help to facilitate the believers' finding the most appropriate way to live.

In any case, perceived beauty in nature is not a simple function of getting what we want, as when we are thirsty in the mountains, of course. Flowers and butterflies lack such obvious intrinsic value for us, yet we all see beauty in them. The beauty of sunrise and sunset, while richly associated with cycles essential to life, is enjoyed in simple observation. On the other hand, essential to life as water is, it also can drown, and in floods and tidal waves it is vastly destructive. Saltwater is unpalatable. And bolts of lightning can be spectacularly beautiful, though life threatening and terrifying.

Some individuals seem oblivious to beauty not directly related to satisfying some desire. I don't know what natural beauty may hold for them. I realize the concept of natural beauty, and our relationship with it, is very complex, still elusive in my casual reflection.

Tuesday morning I left the lake behind as I continued my trek, musing about beauty. The trail led through brushy terrain across several crest saddles, affording delightful views of glaciated canyons and basins holding a series of lakes.

The day before I was to meet Zhita at Carter Meadows Summit, I came upon another marshy area with plentiful pitcher plants. I picked a couple of the plants to show Zhita, and in the base of the tubular stem of one of them I found a dead fly on its way to being digested in the submerged tubular network which connected the interlocking plants with their roots. I carefully retrieved the fly with a twig and inserted it into the root tube to continue to its destiny. Then I placed the two pitcher plants on the wide brim of my hat.

When I arrived at the parking lot beside the trail at the summit, Zhita was talking to two women who were out for a drive, having stopped briefly to enjoy the view. I showed them the lush green plants I was carrying on my hat brim, and they assured me that the pitcher plant was very common in the area, though not common outside of these mountains. One of the women even told us the Latin name of the species, *Darlingtonia Californica*. I had hiked about 80 miles then, making my total for the year almost 240 miles.

Zhita noted that I was exhausted that day, especially after I had my second beer. Shower, food, and rest were all most welcome. Saturday morning in our motel in Weed I cleaned my gear and repacked with the next week's supplies. We drove to Seiad Valley to check out the place we were to meet after the following week's hike, and later we drove to Shasta City for dinner at the restaurant I had visited with Gene and Claire.

Sunday morning we were off to an enthusiastic start, as I was about to hike my last full week in California to the foot of the mountains leading into Oregon. Driving back to Carter Meadows Summit on a nicely paved but narrow and winding forest road, we rounded a curve to find a rock lying in our way. Startled, Zhita drove the car over the rock, unable to swerve around it. There was a sickening sound as the car came to an abrupt halt. Looking underneath the Prius I could see that the exhaust system was badly damaged, but we were now clear of the rock. I moved the car forward then rolled the rock off the road. After discussing our options I decided to abort my hike and try to drive slowly to the nearest Toyota dealer. I could not leave Zhita alone with the problem.

Zhita made some phone calls as I drove, and she found that the nearest Toyota dealer was in Redding. Since it was Labor Day weekend, the dealer's service department would not be open until Tuesday. I drove about 25 mph on Interstate 5 with the guttural exhaust roaring and hazard lights flashing all the way back to Redding. We kept the windows open in case exhaust fumes leaked into the car.

We had to stay in Redding almost a week while parts were brought in and the car repaired. While we waited we explored the town and surrounding area, discovering a dramatic pedestrian suspension bridge designed by Calatrava, the Spanish architect, leading to a lovely park. When the car was ready, my hike schedule was about used up, so I decided to do just a small makeup hike in southern California to see the piece of trail which I had skipped at the end of my first year. On Thursday we headed for home.

Zhita

On August 30, eleven days since I left him at the trail, I prepare to meet Jim again. I pack up with joy at the prospect of our meeting, and start on my way. The temperature outside is extremely hot—99-106 degrees! But the air in the car is wonderfully cool. I stop at Williams, a town that is hardly there—nothing but motels, two restaurants, and a nearby casino. Stay in a motel that night, then drive to Weed (I love the name) and on to the trail. I find it just as described. I'm a bit concerned that Jim is not there, but he soon appears. Pooped! But he is there! We drive to our motel in Weed, and after two beers, Jim is even more pooped, but it is wonderful to be together. This time Jim stays off the trail for two nights so we have time to do a little eating, exploring and just relaxing together—a real plus for both of us.

On September 2, we begin the day with great enthusiasm. We both pack up and head for the trail. I am driving and enjoying the scenery as we drive—until I turn round a bend on one of the roads and immediately confront a rock in my path. No time to swerve, especially with the possibility of oncoming traffic. Imagining/hoping that I can clear the rock, I drive over it. Crunch! Halt! Misery.... You've heard the rest from Jim. And while it was a disappointment for him, I must confess that our stay in Redding was actually a plus for me. I got to be with my husband and spend days of leisure and sightseeing together. The car was damaged—but repaired—and we would be able to continue.

On September 6, we finally leave Redding and head for home. September 7 is a Friday, and Friday Night of each week has long been a very special time for us. Our Friday Night tradition began at the end of the first week that we were married. Each of us had been at work all week and looked forward to the weekend as a time to finally relax together. I came home and prepared a small feast that would begin with hors d' oeuvres, include a sumptuous entrée, and end with dessert, always one of my absolute requirements. Jim fixed Manhattans, my favorite cocktail, which he had learned to make since he knew me. We sat down in the living room with its big picture window to enjoy our cocktails and hors d' oeuvres as we savored our time together. By the time we had finished this first course, we were both pretty full. The entrée seemed superfluous; it could wait for another evening. But, for me, dessert is a must... so we had dessert. It was a wonderful evening, and it became our Friday night tradition—Manhattans, hors d' oeuvres, and dessert—and it continues to this day. So, of course, on September 7, we had a Friday Night, and we reviewed our calendars for the coming year. Jim, noting that our 25th anniversary was coming up in March, proposed another wild and wonderful idea for our celebration: We would go on an Elderhostel cruise of the Middle East! What an exciting plan! That's my beloved....

Jim

Zhita cheerfully adjusted her plans to accommodate my makeup hike. Saturday, September 8 we drove to the Mill Creek Summit Ranger Station in Angeles National Forest where I had bailed out in 2004 with my sore shin muscles. Now I set out to hike through the skipped section to the town of Agua Dulce, at long last. At Messenger Flats Campground in the late afternoon I met a Forest Ranger who was driving on a nearby dirt road. I had discovered that the water in the campground was shut off, so I was glad the ranger offered me some of the water that he was carrying. He said he was involved in fighting a wildfire not far away. When he learned where I was hiking he took out his map and studied it, showing me where the fire had burned and where it was now heading. He said I would be okay on the PCT, for recently the fire had moved away from the trail. My father had spent his career working for the Forest Service, so the ranger and I talked awhile about that rewarding career.

Setting up camp in the vacant campground was a luxury, with picnic tables to use and tent sites already cleared. I got an early start the next day, and later I came to the North Fork Saddle Ranger Station where I found a young man working on some forest service equipment. When he learned where I was hiking, he warned that the forest ahead of me was closed because of the fire. I told him a ranger had said my hike would be okay, so he took his radio and drove off in an ATV to a ridge from which his radio could reach the man in charge of fighting the fire. I could not see the fire or any burned area from where I waited, and I hopefully refilled my water containers. Soon he returned to say I had permission to continue, the first person to be allowed into the burn. The fire was being fought some distance away, but he cautioned me that there still might be hot coals under the ashes where the PCT went through the freshly burned area. Then he asked me to say hello to the Saufleys in Agua Dulce if I should see them.

I proceeded with caution, grateful for permission to continue hiking rather than having to call Zhita once again to bail me out from the trail. The guidebook pages, map and compass were a great help in navigating through the fresh burn as, at times, I could not see any trail or sign or tree blazes in the ashes and debris. Once I completely lost track of the trail for a while where it was interrupted by a firebreak scoured along a ridge crest. A bulldozer had obliterated all traces of the trail, and of course there were no boot prints or other clues to follow. With my map in hand, I made my way along the ridge until finally I reached a point where the trail reappeared, turning away from the ridge with its long, wide firebreak.

Not long after I had left the burned area behind, I arrived at my final planned campsite, a developed campground beside a forest road. That was not my preferred type of campsite, because easy access by road occasionally drew rowdy campers who were not the type to be hikers. My concern was that alcohol and possibly guns might result in unpredictable and unwelcome behavior - a stereotype, I know, but I was leery of boisterous car campers.

At this campground I found only a quiet couple who were camping near their car. I set up my tent, and then I went across the campground to meet them. We talked about their vacation outing and my hike for that year. Reassured, I asked if I could buy a beer from them. Instead, the man insisted on giving me two beers to enjoy, an unexpected treat. After a welcome shower in the campground's primitive shower stall, I ate my dinner and bedded down for the night.

On Monday I approached Agua Dulce through the fantastic rock formations of Vasquez Rocks County Park, a place Zhita and I had visited together in the past. Millions of years ago an upheaval along an offshoot of the San Andreas Fault left gigantic slabs of red sandstone jutting skyward at 45 degrees, and the trail now winds among them. I reached Agua Dulce at the edge of the park, and for once it was comparatively easy both for Zhita and for me to find our meeting spot. I had hiked the missing link, about 36 miles, for a total of about 275 miles for the year, less than I planned but not bad under the circumstances.

It was an eventful year's hiking. At least only our car had been damaged, and that was now restored.

Zhita

And on the following day, September 8, Jim is ready for the last short hike of this summer. I take him to the trail off the Angeles Crest Highway. It is a beautiful day; he is in good spirits and so am I. I leave him at the trail, and he is trekking again. Phone works the next day, and the news is good; Jim sounds great.

Jim and Zhita Rea

On September 10, I have a pretty wild day of my own. There is just too much going on in my world, but it is all good stuff: One of my League colleagues has arranged for Russian visitors to come to the complex where I live so that I can talk to them about elections in the US. I must also meet with League interns regarding their preparation to be facilitators at our very special annual Running and Winning Forum during which high school students meet in small, informal discussion groups with people who have held elective office to find out from them what it means to run for office, organize a campaign, raise funds, etc.., and I must go to my granddaughter Maya's school in Long Beach where I am a volunteer in her fourth grade classroom. All these things are on my mind and in my plans as I make arrangements to meet Jim—hectic, but all good. So I wrap up those thoughts as I start on my way to meet Jim in Agua Dulce. This time it's an easy meet-up in the majestic Vasquez Rocks Wilderness Area. We have lunch out and head for home. And this time he will stay. Year 2007 ends on a high note, in spite of its mishaps and stresses.

2008 Rescue

**Because of your melodic nature, the
moonlight never misses an appointment.**

MY FAVORITE CHINESE COOKIE FORTUNE

S ure enough, the moon did continue in its orbit while I was on the
trail, though sometimes obscured by clouds having no regard for
my melodic nature. Only I occasionally failed to keep an appointment
on the trail.

I particularly looked forward to my hike in 2008, for I would be hiking
through the northern tip of California and into Oregon, at last. John
would be hiking with me through part of Oregon, and Gene would fly
up for a day hike with me. A special highlight of the final part of this
section would be hiking with Darbi and Kirsten, something we had all
wanted to do together on the PCT. I planned a hearty 400 mile hike for
this year through richly forested mountains, and it would include a visit
to Crater Lake.

I packed all my food and supplies into weekly bags, and my hike
plan, trail guidebook pages, trail data book pages and maps were par-
celed out and ready. I would have to skip the section I had not hiked in
the last week of the previous year after the rock damage to the car, because now the Russian Wilderness was closed to hikers due to wild fires.

I decided to see that section the following year. But with all my plans and preparations, naturally some of the most memorable events of the year were unplanned.

Near the end of July, during the months of training, planning and preparing for my hike I happened to see an article in the Fitness section of the LA Times which I have excerpted here:

> *"A killer temptation – Synthetic EPO was intended to help anemic patients, but it can be deadly when illegally used in sports."*

A large picture showed a crowd of cyclists in the 16th stage of the Tour de France, pedaling uphill in the mountains. Three cyclists had been kicked out of the race for using a synthetic form of EPO, a banned performance enhancing drug. The natural form is "a hormone that stimulates bone marrow to produce red blood cells. Everybody needs this hormone." The article went on to say that synthetic EPO was developed to help patients who don't have enough of the natural hormone and who are therefore anemic, including patients on chemotherapy. But "a number of cyclists have mysteriously died in their hotel rooms… It's suspected that they used too much EPO."

What grabbed my attention in the newspaper article was the following:

"Why do athletes think EPO is so great? Muscles need oxygen to burn glucose to produce energy. The longer and harder they work, the more oxygen they need, and the faster they need it. Red blood cells are the body's oxygen delivery system. They carry it throughout the body. When people are anemic, they get tired easily because their oxygen supply is impaired…. [Athletes] who compete at top levels requiring considerable endurance can benefit from having an extraordinary delivery system. For them, adding extra red blood cells – to a point – is like adding extra UPS trucks at Christmas."

Ordinarily such an article would elicit only my casual interest, but this was no ordinary time for me. Just a few months earlier I had been diagnosed with Polycythemia Vera (PV), a somewhat rare, incurable blood cancer which causes bone marrow to produce too many red blood cells. Red blood cell congestion can cause clotting, heart attacks and strokes, so the treatment is to reduce the volume of red cells (hematocrit) by removing pints of blood as needed and suppressing the overproductive marrow with mild oral chemotherapy. My hematocrit was brought from a dangerous 58% down to 42%, safely in the mildly anemic zone, with the aim of keeping it below 45 thereafter. Blood tests to check that level would be part of my new routine.

The disease is neither contagious nor inherited, so my loved ones would not be affected. I found that I had a disease with no symptoms and a treatment with no significant side effects, and the median survival period with this disease would allow me to live about as long as my parents had lived. No big deal. My life was not affected. Dr. Dubernet, my hematologist, said I need not change my hike plans.

But wait. Hiking 400 miles in the mountains each summer at my modest pace certainly did not compare with the demands of cycling in the Tour de France, but I still found it challenging. Some elite endurance athletes were taking dangerous risks with EPO to get their hematocrit above 50 temporarily to improve performance. (It is one of the drugs Lance Armstrong later admitted to taking.) Surely it would help me while hiking at altitude if my hematocrit were allowed to rise above the anemic level of 42 to something near 50, the normal upper limit for males. That did not seem dangerous to me, though I was aware that because of my age I was at high risk of blood clots and heart attack if my hematocrit was too high.

I did not want Dr. Dubernet to prescribe EPO for me, of course, nor did I want my hematocrit to get dangerously high. But I sent her an email to ask whether she thought it would help me to temporarily reduce my chemo medication from 1000mg to 500mg per day for a few weeks to let my hematocrit rise a little until I completed this year's hike. She replied that my hematocrit of 42 was adequate. "Adequate" was not what I wanted to hear. But I knew this issue was too serious for me to take matters into my inexperienced hands.

I then wrote to Zhita's brother, Howard Nash, a researcher at National Institutes of Health, who had provided me with information about PV. He was both a medical expert and a family member. I couldn't ask for a better advisor. Howard replied unequivocally, "They can keep people alive for 14 years with the standard treatment [for PV]. I wouldn't mess with that." A couple of years later Howard was found to have kidney cancer, and he willingly participated in a couple of clinical trials of experimental new treatments before he died. A man with personal involvement in high stakes medical treatment outside the norm, he never wavered in his support of my sticking to the standard treatment as prescribed by Dr. Dubernet.

That settled it. I didn't know whether my modest endurance challenges might be noticeably affected by experimenting with my medication level, but I wasn't going to mess with it. I would huff and puff as needed, and I would slow down when necessary. But I would hike the PCT.

Zhita's Story 2008

August: A new year of the PCT adventure has begun, and this year we will be prepared. Now we are practiced at this, so we know just what to do. Although there are a few new elements:

Some of the distances between Jim's starting points on the trail and my return to LA are pretty great and it may not be practical for me to plan to return home each week. That sounds like an opportunity for me to do a little exploring of my own in places unfamiliar to me. I like that idea. And so we begin.

On August 7, while Jim is packing up and getting ready, I also do some preparation. Mine involves interviewing the general manager of Park La Brea, the huge apartment community in which we live, in order to write an article for our residents' association newsletter. I also make a trip to Whole Foods and Farmers Market to get stuff for Jim's sustenance on the trail.

On Monday, August 8, we drive off, stopping to visit family before continuing on to Jim's next starting point. On August 9, we drive to the motel in Yreka where I will be spending the next several days. Together we work on more details of the hike plans. A note in my journal is prescient: "Very aware of decline from aging for each of us; really want to help Jim reach his goal safely."

August 10: When I leave Jim at the trail and return to the motel, I immediately get busy with the stuff of my life. I am very active with the League of Women Voters of Los Angeles, initiator and chair of its programs for youth. I am also very involved with the Resident Association at Park La Brea, the huge apartment community in Los Angeles where we live. I am currently in charge of the grievance procedure for residents who have issues that must be resolved with management. And it is important that I manage these responsibilities, even from afar. But, now, in my new temporary setting, I want to take advantage of the opportunities to explore the area. I make time in the afternoon to begin my exploration. I traverse the area by car and on foot and eat lunch in a lovely park area behind my motel. Very peaceful and feeling luxurious; this should be interesting.

August 11: Jim calls, sounding wonderful but a little behind on his schedule. Continuing with my ever-present list of responsibilities, I write an article for the PLBRA Newsletter. I note, "There is something peaceful in communicating from afar. Responsibility is limited; I feel free." And then I go out to explore Yreka. I visit the Old Town with its interesting shops, historic buildings and friendly people. I see a sewing machine for $30—hmmm, should I buy that to use along the way? I explore the Dollar Store, have dinner at the Black Bear Inn. Have my mouth set on meat loaf, but they are out; look forward to bread pudding for dessert, but they don't have any. But, even with the disappointments, I enjoy the luxury of "eating out."

August 12: Jim's early phone call confirms that he is doing well but still trying to catch up to the scheduled miles on his hike plan. I spend an interesting day in Yreka at the quilt shop, the museum with its interesting section on Native Americans, and walking, walking, walking around the town and beyond to its outskirts. But I miss sounds (music, voices) and my dear people. My daughter Deb's always daily calls are now particularly welcome—as we talk about her ups and downs, her insights and growth. I start brainstorming on designs for special quilts for each daughter, a project that I am eager to begin. And tomorrow I will meet my beloved!

Jim

Zhita and I drove to Seiad Valley to start my hike on Sunday, August 10. She noted that there was a smoky haze in the air in Yreka where we stayed the night before and again in the valley when we arrived in the morning, but the waiter who served our breakfast in Seiad Valley said there was no wildfire in the area. I began hiking from the village at Mile 1662.

On my first day, with a full pack on a warm day, I faced a climb of over 4,500 ft, equivalent to hiking out of the Grand Canyon to the South Rim. At least here there were trees to provide shade at times, and the heat in the low 90's wasn't so bad. The elevation I reached was only 5,900 ft, so I did not have any special problem with getting enough oxygen. I did drink all of my water before I could filter more. I met only a few hikers, all southbounders descending from the Oregon border. When I reached that border I signed the trail register as Over the Hill Jim for the first time, trying out my newly adopted trail name.

A Hereford calf adopted me as I hiked through a small meadow the next day. The trail took me near a small group of cows and calves lying in the grass in the late morning sun. One calf must have been hungry and frustrated that its mother would not get up to let it have some milk, I imagined, for it began following me into the forest. I couldn't persuade the calf that I had no milk to offer, and it persisted in following me as closely as it could, nuzzling me as a hint. When I saw that losing sight of its mother was not going to stop the calf, I tried to shoo it away. It moved away only a few feet, then it continued to follow me whenever I started walking. I shouted at the calf, hoping its mother might show some concern and come to the rescue, but neither calf nor cow responded.

Deciding I was not really responsible for this calf, I walked on for about half a mile. Finally I stopped, waved my arms and shouted and then smacked the poor calf repeatedly with my trekking poles. To no avail. In desperation I picked up a freshly fallen tree branch and vigorously chased the calf back toward its mother. When the calf finally retreated away from me back down the trail, I turned and practically ran to get away. At last the calf did not follow. I could only hope that it would continue back on the trail to find its mother. Otherwise, I feared, it would die out there alone.

Hiking down the slopes to Ashland was easier, but I was pushing myself to keep on my schedule. Meeting Zhita turned out to be a bit tricky, even though I had planned to meet her at Mt. Ashland Inn. When we met, I was so exhausted that I wasn't up to going out for dinner, though I had hiked only about 60 miles. The next day I felt fine.

Zhita

August 13: After a scenic drive to the area, I check into a motel and drive out to Mt. Ashland Inn to scope out the site where I am to meet J. The owner of the inn emphasizes that I cannot park in his lot, driveway, etc., and points out that there is no parking on the highway. He refers me to the PCT parking lot about two miles up the road, so I drive to check it out and return to the motel.

At about 5pm, I set out again. I go the PCT parking lot and wait anxiously because I know that the meeting place is not clear. When my cell phone rings, I see that it is Jim, but the signal is so weak, I cannot hear him. Somewhat frantic, because I know that his message must be important, I drive down the hill in search of better reception. I have a message from Jim describing his location. Again, I try to call—and this time, I reach him! He describes where he is, but I am very puzzled. I keep driving in what seems like the logical direction; and—wonder of wonders—he is there! Very tired, clearly stretched, and voice nasal. But he is here!

We drive to the motel. While he cleans up. I go to a nearby restaurant for gourmet take-out dinner; then walk across the road to the grocery for beer and bananas. We have a very pleasant meal at the tables on the deck of the motel, but I am concerned about J. Hope he wakes refreshed.

August 14: Jim sleeps well and looks like his usual perky self. He packs up and gets ready to get back on the road. We drive to the trail; so easy when we're together and we know where we're going. So wonderful to have hugs—and I will meet him on the trail again tomorrow.

I come back to Ashland and go to the Laundromat to wash Jim's clothes. I am amazed at how clean they get, even though I forgot to spray them with Shout. It's a very, very hot day (100 degrees plus). After lunch, I get set to do my work. I start the computer and have problems with the Internet connection—familiar but frustrating—but the problem is finally resolved.

Then I decide to go to Hyatt Lake to see if I can locate tomorrow's meeting place. I have no trouble finding the lake; the big problem is finding the PCT crossing. I try numerous different paths, stop lots of folks to ask for advice. Finally, after more than an hour of searching, I notice a park office that I had completely overlooked before. The employee who comes out to help says, "No problem." I am just around the corner from the inconspicuous PCT marker. To add a note of excitement, I spy a notice about a cougar that has been spotted in the area. I also speak to an eccentric but very nice old guy who is much concerned about the cougar. I just pray that J and cougar keep great distance from each other.

Reassured about the meeting place, I go back to the motel ready to find a pleasant place for dinner. No luck.... Almost all the restaurants are in the theater district. I'd rather save that experience to share with J on Saturday night. I wander around, very disappointed, and wind up at a Wendys! Very sad....

Jim

Due to a quirk in the proximity of the trail to the town and surrounding communities together with the locations of other likely resupply places, I returned to the trail to hike just two more days before meeting for another resupply. The temperature was over 100 degrees.

I had planned to meet Zhita at about 5:00 on Saturday. However I called her to ask for a lunch date, for I had hiked the 29 miles in a day and a half and arrived at Hyatt Lake by noon. We went to the café at the lake and had an outrageous pizza for lunch. She told me about a warning notice she had seen about a cougar in the area, and I was concerned about my poor calf. Powerless to help, I wishfully urged the critter to stay with its mama.

Violent encounters between hikers and cougars or bears on the PCT were so rare that I had decided from the beginning to hike without a spray can of bear repellent. Reading more about such encounters several years later, I decided that if I hiked again in such terrain I would carry the added weight of a spray can just in case.

I was scheduled to have a blood test every six weeks, and it was time for another one. I had previously determined online that the Ashland Community Hospital had a lab which could do the blood test for me, so we went there on my day off. I learned that my hematocrit was 39.9 in that test. Did I only imagine that hiking was harder? Probably, for the performance benefit of a dangerously high hematocrit above 50 was said to be only 1% for an elite athlete. Mild anemia could not be much of an excuse for me. Ah well.

Zhita

When I return to the motel room, I have trouble finding my cell phone, but I recover it quickly, only to note with dismay that I have a message. It's from Jim asking me if I'd like to have a lunch date with him. He had covered the 11+ miles and was at his destination by noon! I call him to say I'll be right there—and, since I don't have to grope for the location, I am right there—in about a half hour and just in time for lunch. What joy!

We go to the café at the lake where I had stopped the day before to get help with finding the PCT destination. We order an outrageous pizza, eat it outrageously, then head for the motel. J collapses unwashed and sleeps about 30 minutes. After a trip to the hospital for J's necessary blood test and dinner at a Mexican restaurant with outrageous Margaritas, we go back to the motel to look at J's photos. J collapses and is snoring peacefully as I write.

August 16: J spends a good part of the day re-packing and resting. In the morning, I decide to go for a walk. A few blocks from the motel, in a lovely shaded area, is a cemetery. Many of the stones identify people born in the early or mid 1800s; very pleasant strolling among them. Ironically, Deb calls as she and Maya are on their way to the cemetery in Long Beach to visit with Poppa, Maya's Grandpa and Deb's father-in-law. Life has such unexpected connections.

August 17: This morning I take J back to the trail. He is in good spirits and seems well rested. Each time I leave him, I am so aware of our mortality; Friday, our next meeting day, seems so far away....

I take a long walk; feels good to get my body moving. I note with pleasure that climbing the stairs to my room is surprisingly less painful than it has been. And then I realize that I have several hours of free time—a rare treat. I decide to sew. In the evening, another rare treat-
-the Ansells, friends from our days in the Long Beach ACLU, who now live in Tucson, have just arrived in Ashland, and they will be leaving tomorrow. I decide to spend an extra night here so that I can see them. Barbara has been quite ill and Mitch also has had some recent medical

problems; both have lost lots of weight but are in good spirits. I meet them at their B&B and we walk to dinner, then walk some more and listen to an outdoor 60s style concert, stop for ice cream at the famous Zoey's. Very pleasant time; so good to see them.

August 18: On the road again to Springfield to dear friend Ann's place. Ann is away, but I am fortunate to be able to stay at her lovely home on a hill overlooking the Willamett River and the countryside. I immediately go to the balcony to enjoy the gorgeous view, but the gray skies—and perhaps the loneliness—trigger the depression gloom that is a recurring part of me. I drive around to explore, eat dinner out, and do some grocery shopping. I return to the house to find a bag of muffins made by Aletha, Ann's wonderful landlady who lives in the house on the lower part of the hill. She has even included a list of ingredients, just in case I might have allergies.

August 19: J's call is so welcome. He is less exuberant but says he is doing fine. I walk to the Springfield Public Library to check my email because they have WiFi. It works fine for a while, then starts acting up. I stay to read Sunday's New York Times. What a treat! We may have to start subscribing. When I leave, I check out the Visitor Center to get some more information about the town, then go out to explore.

August 20: J calls about 8:30; sounds good and is on track. I drive to Portland to spend the day with my cousin Deborah. She is a much younger cousin whom I really like but seldom see. Her daughter Sophie joins us. We sit and visit at her very interesting home, then go to the Hands On Café at the College of Arts and Crafts, where the delicious food is prepared by students. We browse the wonderful gift shop admiring its wares made by staff and alumni of the school. Then Deborah and I go walking on a trail in one of the lovely parks. There is a light rain but the trees are a shield and everything is gorgeously green. In the evening, we go for supper and dessert at PIX. The most gorgeous desserts I have ever seen.

Deborah and I continue talking about this stage of her life, about Sophie who has just returned from a year in Spain and will now be a senior in high school, about Sid who is a senior at Tempe, Arizona. I feel very old… I drive home through intermittent showers and see the most vivid rainbow that I have ever seen!

August 21: Ann is home. We talk to catch up a bit, then each of us goes our separate ways to run the necessary errands. In the evening, daughter Wendy calls to tell me about granddaughter Zhita Lynne's success on her academic test after she attended the school's tutoring sessions. We are all proud of ZZ!

Jim

For the next week I hiked in grandly forested Oregon, with the usual occasional rain. There were few opportunities to see any scenery beyond the forest surrounding me, but it was a pleasant setting in lush contrast with the deserts back in the Southwest.

As I approached Crater Lake I left the official, horse-approved PCT trail which avoids the lake, and I made my way on the hikers' alternative Dutton Creek Trail toward the lake. Passing the village and then some great views of the lake, I found our meeting site just north of the Rim Drive, having hiked 90 more miles. Zhita was not there. She had found a large PCT sign on the road about two miles south of the rim drive, but that did not match my directions to our meeting site. When she found a place that did match, there was no PCT sign. After she searched for a couple of hours, I was able to reach her cell phone briefly to describe where I was. She left the PCT trailhead parking area she was in (which we later learned was for equestrians), and she found me soon after. We had something to eat in the village and then made the 100 mile drive to our motel in Roseburg.

While I was reorganizing the next day, Zhita reads, quilts, then goes out to buy a jug of water to cache and some iron-on patches for another hole in my pants. On our way back to Crater Lake we stopped to find a spot to cache water at the Crater Lake trailhead off of Highway 138.

Over the Hill

We briefly viewed the beautiful lake, which we had not seen in many years, and returned to the trail at the unmarked spot where we had previously met. There we found a young woman hiker who was working on a through-hike of the PCT, and she was heading north. We talked with her briefly and learned that Rock Star was her trail name. Rock Star continued hiking north, while Zhita and I called our friend Milan in Los Angeles to wish him a happy one hundredth birthday. I said I was sure that this must be his first satellite phone call for his birthday, and he assured me that it was. We wished Milan and his beloved wife Shanta well.

Zhita and I parted with hugs and kisses. I started hiking, and before long I met up with Rock Star. We started talking, and by the end of the day she decided to slow her pace to match my 14 to 17 miles per day for a while for the sake of having someone to talk to. That afternoon we found my water cache and refilled with "easy water." Rock Star smiled to see the flattened container tied to my pack. On the second day she decided to continue hiking with me until we met Zhita again. I said she could ride with us then to Eugene, which would be convenient for her. She had been hiking about 25 miles each day, so this change of pace would mean that she would have only snack food to eat for dinner a couple of evenings before resupplying on Saturday. Rock Star decided that was okay.

We soon encountered colder weather and pouring rain. With a break in the rain late Tuesday, we took advantage of a fire ring and made a campfire, my first while hiking the PCT. Unfortunately, Rock Star developed a severe toothache the morning after her cold dinner, and she left the trail to go to Shelter Cove so she could hitch a ride to a dentist.

On my way up a long gradual climb on the trail I met a young man hiking north. Eric told me he hiked on the PCT for a week each year, and he was very interested to hear about my series of hikes. He slowed his pace to walk with me. After a couple of hours I stopped to take a break, and Eric walked on. On Thursday, two days later, I met Zhita at

Charlton Lake, and we drove to Springfield to stay with our friend Ann. I had hiked another 90 miles.

Zhita

August 22: Ann wakens refreshed and much more herself. I prepare to meet J. Drive to Crater Lake on Hwy 138 along the Umqua River; gorgeous area. Of course, there is drama about identifying the exact meeting place. There is a large PCT sign and parking lot about two miles south of the Rim Drive, but that location does not match J's directions. The place that does match does not have a PCT sign. Dilemma renewed.... I drive around the Rim Drive—down to the Village, up the hills, back to the parking lot—for about two hours, just searching. Then I get a call from J with a snatch of description before the phone goes out. Since I am at the PCT parking lot and he is obviously not there I drive back to the Rim and arrive just as he is coming down the hill. I honk; he notices; we meet. Stunning embrace—another drama on the PCT. J has a cold beer which I have brought and we begin the 100-mile drive to the motel. Back at the motel, he restores and refreshes. As always, so wonderful to be together again.

August 23: J works on reorganizing. I read, enjoy quilting. I go out to buy a bottle of water for Jim to cache, then explore the shops around the motel. In the evening, during our dinner at Applebee's, each of us gets a call—Kirsten for J, Deb for me. We each leave the table to talk on our cell phones; who, in our generation, would ever have imagined? Back at the motel, J and I pore over maps to determine our next meeting place. Fortunately, he has a new copy of the PCT map, and I make a copy of the map from his PCT book. Looks clear; let's hope....

August 24: Wake at 6, leave motel by 7:30. Drive to Crater Lake, stopping on the way for J to cache the water. Long hugs as he starts on the trail again. I drive to Rim Village with many stops to take in the spectacular scenery. Continue on to Roseburg and to Ann's. In the evening, Ann and I try to watch the Olympics: channel not working, but we can get CNN for news of the Democratic convention. Obama has chosen Joe Biden as his running mate.

August 25: J calls, sounds great. I do laundry, email, back to Valley Center Mall to get PCT Day Hikes book for J and me, then back for a long walk in the late afternoon. Ann and I spend another evening with the Democrat's convention. Tonight Ted Kennedy makes a remarkably strong presentation; amazing, considering that he has just had surgery to remove a brain tumor. Michelle Obama is a powerful speaker.

August 26: J calls late and I am very anxious, but he sounds fine. He reports that Rock Star has decided to slow her pace as a through-hiker and stay with him for company. Should make for interesting conversation when he returns. ☺

A day of errands—check out motel where J and I will stay with Jim's brother John who will be joining Jim for the next part of the trek. I get gas, go to the car wash, Safeway, Trader Joe.... Getting to know my way around the area.

In the evening, Ann's landlady Aletha comes by with vegetables from her garden and homemade muffins. She is a delight. Ann and I spend another evening with the Democratic convention. This evening Hillary gives a speech, as I enjoy my quilting.

August 27: J calls about 9am. Gives me info about his revised hiking route. He and Rock Star are hiking together and she would like a ride to Eugene when I pick J up. I think her being with him has added some tension for Jim; he does not sound joyous when he calls. Saddens me.

I work on the computer—some success and some frustration. I talk to Deb and Wen. Wen talks about her job at school, complications regarding her planned mission trip to India, ZZ's being "horrible" (i.e., temperamental) and the inspired way that Greg responds by getting her to communicate in writing at the beginning of each day. Good to have this opportunity for dialog with daughters.

In the afternoon, I go to the art gallery that promotes local artists and has special opportunities for kids from poor families. I also go to the History Museum where they have a display of clothing from eastern

Europe—gorgeous embroidery, elaborate decoration. Then proceed to the history of Springfield end of the museum.

Ann and I go out to talk to the computer guy. Sounds like he thinks the laptop may have serious problems. Later, I go out to find dessert, one of the essentials of my well being. I discover a wonderful little place that has delicious brownies; what a find! Tonight the Democratic convention features Bill Clinton and Joe Biden, both of whom give great speeches; all are at their finest. Obama will have a challenge to take it up from there. (I quilt while watching.) Ann retires early, and I get back to the computer to respond to an email about some happenings at Park La Brea. More challenges to deal with long distance; surprisingly, there is comfort in knowing that I am far away—and, therefore, my sense of responsibility for resolving all the problems is reduced. I have a legitimate excuse....

Deb calls. She has had a good day visiting with friends Missy and Christine, visiting Christine's bistro and food preparation shop. She also has gotten a handle on the issues related to Maya's teacher and has an appointment with the principal tomorrow. Life is full and good....

August 28: Slept poorly last night. Awake several hours—stressed about J, computer mess, LWV responsibilities .... Wake at 8; J calls shortly after. Sounds much more relaxed; I am much relieved.

Today Ann helps me figure out some of the computer woes; stuff I had sent to the League office worked fine. I send some more info. Ann arranges for us to have dinner with Jane, the mother of Ann's daughter-in-law Amy, who has recently moved here. We go to a restaurant on the river, sit outside—beautiful. Back at the house we listen to Obama's acceptance speech. Terrific! I quilt. Then we drive Jane home. Good day.

August 29: Today is Retrieve Jim Day. No call till after 10am. Makes me a little uneasy, but I stay occupied. Gorgeous scenery en route and, lo-and-behold, all roads are properly marked. Find the place easily. I wait more than an hour but am grateful to see "Viejo" trudging the unpaved road.... Big, sweaty hugs, then drive back to Ann's. J's usual clean-up and nap routines before enjoying gorgeous views.

August 30: John arrives by car at about 2pm. Instead of asking him to find his way around town, we rescue him from the Safeway parking lot and go to the motel where the three of us will spend the night. In the afternoon, John discovers that he has left his hiking clothes, directions, contact information, etc. at home. I go to Fred Myers to find "light blue shirts that do not need ironing," as he specifies.

August 31: Up at 6am to get the guys to the trail. We drive up to Charlton Lake. This time I drive the unpaved road—not too bad. It's a chilly day—36 degrees when I drop the guys off. I hate to let go of my love.

On the way back, I stop at a covered bridge and read all the info in the interpretive center. The cover is to protect the bridge. Seeing the huge planks, I try to imagine how the workers handled them. Very interesting; another remarkable story....

The house is so empty. I go for a walk up City View and around to the park at the summit of the hill, then down to Island Park; pleasant places. Back at the house, I cut flowers from the garden. Such a joy! Then do some computer stuff, laundry, read papers. Feel very lonesome. During the late afternoon, I hear surprising sounds and realize it is pouring. Sure hope it doesn't affect the guys on the trail.

Jim

Zhita dropped us off at Charlton Lake. John and I made our way through dense pine forest initially, and we hiked four miles farther than my plan called for. It began to rain as soon as our tents were up.

We maintained our four mile advantage for the rest of the week in the beautiful Three Sisters Mountains area. When we reached the creek and meadow where I planned to camp on our last night on the trail together, we met a young hiker who told us there was a good place to camp on top of a small rise beside the trail. His tent was up there, and he said there was plenty of room for more. We found pleasant spots among the trees, so we set up our tents.

Talking as we set up camp, filtered water and prepared our dinners, we learned that John Freeman was an interesting and amiable man who had decided to hike the PCT through Oregon and then hitch a ride to Portland. He knew a girl who lived there, and he was going to see her. He had gotten a pack and loaded up, vacating his apartment in Bend and walking north at a comfortable pace. In a pleasant spot like the one we were in, he would camp for an extra day or two. He told us that his maternal grandmother was full-blooded Lakota Indian. His mother now lived in Florida, and his father lived in Alaska where John had lived for quite a few years.

Since both my brother and Freeman were named John, I started calling them Brother John and Lakota John. We spent a pleasant evening together, and next morning Lakota John told us he really enjoyed listening to me and my brother talking. He had lost his own older brother in an accident years ago, and hearing my brother and me brought back good memories.

Brother John and I prepared for our day's hike to McKenzie Pass at Highway 242 where we would meet Zhita. Since it was our last day on the trail before my resupply, we gave Lakota John our extra food. Saying goodbye, Lakota John said he might see me again farther up the trail. I would be taking a day off from hiking, and I agreed that we might well see each other again. That day we encountered even more volcanic flows as well as numerous obsidian deposits, shiny black volcanic glass fragments in abundance. This was very different terrain from what we had seen in previous years while together on the PCT.

We met Zhita at McKenzie Pass on Wednesday afternoon and drove back to Springfield. We took Brother John with us to the motel where we cleaned up and rested a bit before going out for dinner. We had hiked together about 60 miles, and once again John hated to leave me on the trail. Very early next morning he headed for home, and after sunrise Zhita and I rose and returned to Ann's house to organize and pack. Gene flew in to the Eugene airport that day, so we met him and had lunch together at the airport. We took him to our motel where I then reworked the hike plan for the next day. Hiking on barren rough rock through lava flows where John and I left off did not seem like an appealing or representative hike on the PCT in Oregon for Gene, so I used the guidebook to find road access to the trail farther north of where John and I had ended our hike together.

Next morning Gene and I began hiking south from the Old Santiam Wagon Road in a dense Oregon pine forest. We hiked together for several miles, and then Gene returned to the trailhead where Zhita waited. I continued hiking south into the lava fields and down to McKenzie Highway near the pass and the Dee Wright Observatory. Zhita and Gene met me there, and she noted that I was exuberant for I had hiked that day with only a day pack. I decided to scrutinize my pack contents next year in another attempt to reduce the weight. We drove back to where Gene and I had begun hiking south, now to drop me off with my full backpack to resume hiking north. Zhita then returned Gene to the motel in Springfield before she returned to Ann's house. Saturday morning she took Gene back to the airport for his flight to Los Angeles, joining him for breakfast at the airport restaurant.

I awoke on the trail on Monday, September 8 at the beginning of what promised to be an exciting week. Darbi was flying in from Albuquerque and Kirsten was driving up from San Francisco for a symbolic family adventure together on my PCT trek. Tomorrow Zhita would bring them to join me at Breitenbush Lake to hike with me for the last three days of this year's hike.

At midday I met Steve and Debbie, section hikers who lived in Oregon. They were heading south and had stopped for lunch. We talked for twenty minutes or so about our experiences on the PCT, and then I continued. A little later I met Susan and her dog Mia, day hiking from their base camp beside Pamelia Lake just off the PCT. Susan was a nurse who loved the outdoors, and we talked about hiking in this area in Oregon and about the PCT. Near the end of the day I noted the Woodpecker Ridge Trail sign, and about a mile later I stopped for the night beside a large unnamed pond at the base of an old rock slide at the foot of a mountain. I later learned this was Mt. Jefferson, and Jefferson Park was not far ahead.

The ground was pretty rocky among the tall pine trees, but I found an adequate campsite a little closer to the trail than I liked. It was a beautiful area, and I sometimes watched the pond in vain for signs of fish feeding on bugs. For dinner I ate a home-prepared meal using dried seafood which Darbi had sent me from Hawaii. The seafood smelled a little bit stale, but I decided it was okay.

After an uneventful night, I got up at about 6:00 on Tuesday. I had my usual breakfast and began preparing my stuff to go in the pack. But at about 7:00 I felt a sharp pain in my abdomen which quickly became severe. I tried different postures and massaging my belly in a vain attempt to ease the pain. I began to suspect that I might have food poisoning from the dried seafood which had not smelled quite right the night before. I also imagined it might be appendicitis. My brother once had acute appendicitis when he was in the Air Force in Vietnam, a serious close call for him. By 8:15 I decided that something important but unidentifiable was wrong with me and it wasn't going away. I had never experienced so much pain, and I needed to see a doctor. I could not hike out in this condition, even without a pack.

I got out my sat phone and found an opening among the towering pines where I could get a signal. Luckily I was able to reach Zhita in Springfield right away, and I told her my plight. I needed a Search and Rescue team to carry me out to a road and get me to a doctor as soon as possible. I could hardly bear to say all this to her, knowing the anxiety it was going to cause. I told her I was at PCT trail mile 2037, about one trail mile north of the Woodpecker Ridge Trail and about 11 trail miles south of Breitenbush Lake, which the guidebook said was a popular fishing spot accessible by Skyline Road 42. That should pinpoint my location for anyone who had a map showing the PCT. I had no idea how to reach a SAR team in Oregon, so we agreed that she should start by calling 911 to ask for help.

Zhita
My Log of Jim's Crisis on the Trail:
September 9:

8:15am—Jim calls in great pain; thinks he has food poisoning! Gives me details of his location—at mile 2035.8 on the PCT; was at Woodpecker Trail last night; hiked downhill beside pond. I immediately call 911. Since Jim was not in town, I was told to call the sheriff of Lane County. Person who answers doesn't seem to know anything about the PCT, checks and tells me to call Linn County. Linn County tells me to call Deschutes County.

9:45am—Finally reach an understanding person who listens, understands the emergency and takes charge—even though it's not in his county. Neil Mackey in Deschutes County Sheriff's Office will call Search and Rescue; and Search and Rescue will call me. He gives me his pager number for further contact. On a subsequent call, he tells me that Marion County SAR Sgt. Sherbourne will call Jim and track him. Then Deputy Klein from Linn County calls to ask for Jim's Kaiser number; they want to check on Jim's medical condition, specifically his polycythemia vera. I don't have the number! I call my daughter Wendy who races home and gets it for me.

10:25am—Woeful, thinking about J; feeling helpless. Thinking about by loved ones—daughters, grandkids, and how precious they are to me. Deb calls, knowing nothing about all this, to ask about J! She says she just had this feeling....

12:45pm—Doug Garrett, Marion County Sheriff's office: He will get a National Guard helicopter with a flight surgeon. Also, Linn and Marion County rescue teams will go on foot. They will be calling Jim on his satellite phone every 15 minutes, then call me.

1:00—National Guard has spotted Jim; medic will stay with him. Sgt. Sherbourne, who has stayed involved, comments on Jim's "great satellite system."

3:00—Jim is finally airlifted to Salem Hospital. Seven hours of torture—for Jim—and for those of us who love him.... By this time, Darbi and Kirsten had arrived, and the three of us left for Salem—on a very different mission from the family hike that Darbi and Kirsten had looked forward to.

That was what I recorded at the time. Seven hours of uncertainty, waiting and waiting, helpless to do anything else—and unaware of the severity of the problem. Thoughts of losing my beloved was, fortunately, beyond my ken. Being by his side, holding his hand were essential. That was my agenda.

Lessons Learned:

1. Jurisdiction and responsibilities of rescue agencies are by county; know what county J calls from.
2. Carry emergency info for J at all times: Kaiser number, meds that he takes, doctors and phone numbers.
3. Find out how best to contact emergency services. Obviously, a call to 911 is not all it takes.
4. Daughters should have basic info about both of us (as in #2)
5. Bring photos of family—just for our joy.

Jim

Once I had called for help, I found some relief sitting where I could lean against a tree or lean forward with my head between my knees. I thought about my newly adopted trail name, Over the Hill Jim, and I wondered now just how literally apt that name might turn out to be. Then I decided that I needed to get my tent and remaining gear back into my pack. A SAR team would not want to spend time gathering it up, and I wouldn't want them to delay getting me to a doctor. The pain eased at times, so I set to work in spurts when I could manage. I finished packing as the hours passed. I worried about what was happening inside me while I packed and then waited, sometimes in a fetal position on the ground. When the deputy sheriff called, believe me I was ready.

I described to the deputy what I was feeling and where I was. When he asked if anyone else was with me I said no. A few other hikers had passed by and offered to help, but I thanked them and explained that I had already called for SAR. The deputy said they prefer to have someone stay with the person waiting to be rescued, so I told him I would ask the next hiker I saw to wait with me.

Only a few minutes later I heard a man's voice calling my name! When I called back to answer, he asked if I was okay. It was Lakota John, hurrying to find me. Some southbound hikers had asked him if he was with SAR, saying that a man with a white beard was in trouble ahead and waiting for rescue. When they confirmed that the man wore a hat with a shiny top, John guessed that it was me, so he was looking for me. He readily agreed to wait with me until someone came to carry me out.

When another deputy called, he told me that one SAR team was setting out from Linn County heading north to look for me and another team was setting out from Marion County heading south. I thanked him. He also called the National Guard. The team that found me was the Guard in a Blackhawk helicopter. The Guard crew saw Lakota John waving my hat with its shiny mylar top and they saw me feebly waving while seated on the ground, but they didn't think we looked desperate. After they roared off to look further, I got a call from the deputy. I told him the helicopter had found us but then flew away, so he said he would send them back. Soon they returned, hovering as they looked for some clearing where they could land. It was about 2:00 in the afternoon. They could not land the helicopter nearby, so they hovered well above the tree tops. When I saw the medic being lowered from the helicopter on a cable, I asked John to bring my camera so I could snap a quick picture.

When the medic stepped off the cable attachment onto the ground, he signaled the crew to hoist the cable and move to a safer altitude. He talked to me about my pain and examined me quickly. Unable to determine the cause of the pain, he guessed that I might have a gallstone. Without positive identification of the problem, he could not give me anything to relieve the pain. I gritted my teeth. We agreed that I should be taken to a hospital right away, so he called the helicopter back. They could not make the cable hoist work, so they gained some altitude again and worked on the hoist. Just as one of them radioed the medic to say they would call for another helicopter, another crew member got the hoist working. They returned to hover above the treetops and lowered the cable.

The attachment on the cable end looked like a steel anchor, except that the three prongs flattened out horizontally from the shaft. The medic had me sit on two of the prongs and hold the shaft, and he slipped a strap around me under my arms, clipping the ends of the strap to the top of the shaft. That was my safety belt, a loose fit but adequate if I kept my arms down by my side. He then attached my pack and my trekking poles to the anchor and even tied my hat to the pack (the prop wash would be very strong). Finally he asked me if I was afraid of heights!

Fortunately I'm not. (Later I wondered what he would have done if I were afraid.) The medic stood on the other prong of the anchor, grasped the cable with one hand, and signaled the crew. Clearly he was not afraid of heights. We began our ascent. As we were hoisted above the treetops and neared the helicopter I let go with one hand and waved goodbye to Lakota John, keeping my arm low to hold the safety strap. When we reached the top of the hoist we were right beside the helicopter with its side door open wide. The crew swung the hoist arm into the craft, so I did not have to try any maneuver over open space. Safely inside, they told me we were about equally close to Salem and to Bend, both of which had a hospital. I was eager to go to Salem, as that was where Zhita was planning to bring my daughters that day en route to where they planned to begin hiking with me.

Being hoisted above the treetops and then flying over the mountains and on to Salem was a spectacular ride. I later told Zhita and the girls what I thought at the time, that it was better than any E Ticket ride at Disneyland in the early days. But with that pain in my belly and my fears about its cause, even an E Ticket ride wasn't worth my price of admission.

An ambulance was waiting for me at the airport, and they whisked me away to the hospital. The emergency room crew was expecting me, for as I later learned the Salem TV news program had made an announcement about the rescue of a 72 year old hiker. I was quickly and efficiently checked out in the ER where I was examined and had a CT scan of my abdomen. The CT showed a blocked bowel which was causing the pain. Now, at last, I could have pain medication. I was admitted to the hospital.

Zhita, Darbi and Kirsten came into my room as soon as I was tucked into bed. My daughters and I would not be hiking today, but I sure was glad to see them. I was fitted with an IV for hydration and a tube through my nose to pump out my stomach. That night the daughters went to a motel while Zhita sat by my bed, holding my hand. I slept.

Wednesday morning my daughters returned to my room. Zhita had slept little in the cold hospital room with me the night before. Dr. Marlowe, the surgeon on duty, came in to discuss my condition, with Zhita, Darbi and Kirsten beside me. Dr. Marlowe explained that an X-ray that morning showed that the blockage continued in my small intestine. Given a choice, I elected to wait and see whether the blockage could be cleared without surgery. After the doctor left, Darbi stayed with me while Kirsten and Zhita went out for breakfast. Zhita went back to the motel to nap. In the hospital or out, there were many calls on each of their cell phones to and from family and friends.

The hospital phone rang beside my bed, and I was pleasantly surprised to hear that it was Gary, the guy I had met on the trail the day before my rescue. He and Debbie had seen a newspaper article in Medford about the rescue, and they guessed that explained all the helicopter activity they had heard on the trail. That Blackhawk was pretty loud. Gary managed to get his call through to me at the hospital to find out whether I was the man they had met on the PCT and to ask how I was. He wished me well. We exchanged cell phone numbers so we could get in touch again.

It must have been a quiet time for local news in Oregon. Zhita's cousin called to ask about me because she heard about the rescue of the 72 year old hiker on the NPR radio broadcast in Portland. Later Zhita found an article about the rescue in the Salem newspaper as well. I had my 15 minutes of fame, which I had not sought.

Dr. Marlowe returned Thursday morning. My stomach had been pumped out successfully, but a more detailed CT that morning showed my intestine was still blocked, perhaps by a twisted section. My pain had increased, requiring more medication, and I had developed a fever. A blood test with an elevated white blood cell count showed that I was fighting an infection. Surgery was required to determine conclusively what was happening with my intestines and to fix it. I agreed to the surgery.

The soonest a surgical team and an operating room could be arranged for me was late that night. Dr. Marlowe would not be on duty then, so she introduced me to Dr. Jaecks, the surgeon who would do the procedure. He told me he specialized in minimally invasive laparoscopic procedures, inserting specialized tools and instruments through a small incision to see inside the patient and work on the problem internally. As I understood it, he would be trying to locate and relieve any kinks in my intestine and free the blockage. More invasive surgery might be required if the problem section had to be removed.

The three days my daughters and I had set aside for hiking together expired that day, so differently from what we had planned. In the evening Kirsten drove herself and Darbi back to Springfield. Darbi needed to get to the Eugene airport for her flight home early on Friday, and Kirsten would then drive home. Zhita waited with me.

Late that evening I was wheeled into the operating room, ironically to have surgery on 9/11. Afterwards Dr. Jaecks explained to Zhita that when he inserted a laparoscope into my abdomen, the scope revealed a black loop of small intestine. Gangrene! He quickly set aside the laparoscope and opened an incision from top to bottom of my abdomen.

Then he pulled out 75 centimeters (about 2 ½ feet) of intestine which was black with gangrene and grossly perforated.

As I understood it, my small intestine had somehow adhered in a kink and cut off blood circulation. The cause of the kink was unknown and not related to my hiking. It could have happened anywhere. After reconnecting the healthy ends of intestine, the surgeon and his team had to clean all the remaining mess out of my abdominal cavity to get rid of the infection without tearing apart his resection. In the wee hours of the morning my abdomen was finally stapled back together.

Zhita was waiting when I was wheeled back into my room. Dr. Jaecks came in soon after to describe what he had found inside me and the surgery he had performed. He assured her that I would be okay. She was very appreciative and greatly relieved.

The next day Dr. Jaecks told me I was lucky to be alive, a judgment later confirmed for me by other doctors. He said few people live long enough to get to the extreme condition I was in and fewer survive. My surgery had turned out well, and he expected me to recover fully. As his message sank in, I thought to myself, "I'm alive! I'm so lucky to be alive!" I thanked him warmly, and Zhita did as well. For months after that experience I exclaimed every day, "I'm alive!" I owe my life to the skills and diligence of my rescue team and my medical team and to the loving support of my family and friends, my wife most of all.

Though this was not the adventure we had planned, Zhita, Darbi, Kirsten and I were very glad that we all had been together through this crisis. We were also very glad that none of us had known how close to death I had been until after the surgery was over.

My hospital room was soothingly calm the morning after the surgery. Zhita began calling and emailing our daughters and other family and friends to relate the news that the surgery went well and I was resting comfortably. Soon Dr. Marlowe was pleased to find that I was recovering well, and she ordered all the tubes removed. I was intrigued when the sweet young nurses began asking me hopefully if I was passing gas. It turned out that I would not be released from the hospital until this sign of the normal functioning of my digestive system had returned. I had never imagined that this humble process was an important part of the functioning of a healthy digestive system. A few days later, digestive system returning to normal, Dr. Marlowe released me from the hospital.

At my exit interview with Dr. Jaecks, he saw that I was very intrigued with what he said he observed when he first inserted the laparoscope into my abdomen, so he gave me copies of the pictures he had taken so I could see the gangrene inside me. I was instructed to recuperate in bed for ten more days before returning to the hospital to have the staples removed.

Zhita drove slowly as we returned to Springfield to recuperate at Ann's house. Traveling was painful because of the surgery, so we stopped every hour so I could rest. Ann was very solicitous and helpful, and Zhita and I were both very grateful to be her guests. When Zhita checked our home phone answering machine, she found a message from Susan, the nurse I had met with her dog on the trail. She too saw a news article about the rescue and figured that explained the helicopter activity she heard. She remembered that I lived in Los Angeles, so she called Information to get my home phone number. Her message was that she thought she had met me on the trail the day before the rescue, and she called to find out whether I was that hiker and how I was doing. Zhita called her and told her the story.

Susan lived in Eugene, next to Springfield where I was recuperating. She soon came to Ann's house to see me and meet Zhita, bringing a loaf of homemade bread for us. I assured her that I would return to Oregon to continue my hike, since the doctor said I could expect a full recovery. On her second visit she exclaimed that she wanted to hike with me for a week the following year. With all my good fortune so far I was confident that I would continue my hike, and I enthusiastically agreed that we should hike together. Zhita was pleased that a nurse would hike with me.

When ten days had passed since my surgery, Zhita cautiously returned me to Salem to the hospital. I told the physician assistant who removed the staples that my daughter wanted to keep the staples, so he put them into a plastic bag for me. We returned to Ann's house in Springfield for another day to rest and heal, then began the long drive to LA. We slowly drove to Mt. Shasta, stopping each hour to give me a rest. The next day we drove to Oroville for another night as guests of my cousin Chuck and Bev, then drove on to San Francisco. There we were joined at our motel by Wendy, Greg and young Zhita as well as Kirsten. Kirsten was pleased that I had remembered to save the staples from my belly for her. Next day we drove as far as San Louis Obispo, and on the 28th we finally arrived at home.

The incisions, internal and external, were healed in six weeks, as the surgeon had said. I cautiously resumed exercising, though six months passed before I could do sit-ups. I had one brief recurrence of intestinal blockage, now due to adhesion of scar tissue, but that was cleared without surgery.

I had missed my appointment at Breitenbush Lake, where Darbi and Kirsten were to begin hiking with me, but the improvised meeting turned out to be life-saving. Future appointments are still possible, and I get more opportunities to enjoy the moonlight.

I had hiked about 375 miles this year, almost as much as I had planned – but with more drama. I proved to be Over the Hill only in the better sense and ready for the next one.

2009 Limits

Returning to hike the PCT this year offered the prospect of a triumph, confirming that I had indeed fully recovered from last year's drastic surgery and eagerly trekking all the remaining parts of the trail in California and Oregon. I would enter Washington, within reach of one final year's hike. I planned to return to the Sierras at the beginning of September this time, when the snow would surely have melted and I would be in my best condition for the challenge of hiking at altitude. Kirsten, John and a couple of friends would hike with me through the Sierras. Gene would fly up to Oregon to hike with me for a day. Susan, the nurse I met on the trail last year just before I was rescued, had decided she could take two weeks off from work so she could hike with me through most of Oregon and into Washington. Zhita would meet me every week for a day off. And with all this wonderful companionship, reassuring after last year's rescue, I would still hike 150 miles alone, a part of the experience I looked forward to.

On Sunday, the second of August, Zhita and I returned to Carter Meadow Summit where I had left off in 2007 because of the Prius-meets-rock incident. The wildfires in the Russian Wilderness in 2008 had prevented me from completing the next section that year, and now at last I would be able to see this part of the trail in northern California. Zhita and I reminisced ruefully about that rock as we approached the trail-head. We agreed that we had been through enough drama related to my hike in the last two years, so we resolved to do without any more such events.

I was glad to be back in the mountains, alone and free. The route through the Russian Wilderness and the Marble Mountain Wilderness was in good condition, as the 2008 wildfires had not reached any place I could see from the trail. I had planned days of moderate mileage and altitude changes, so I did not expect real challenges this week. But I found that I got pretty tired by the end of each day, and I had difficulty keeping on schedule.

I had told people that being diagnosed with Polycythemia Vera did not affect my life, my plans and activities – but of course it affected me. "So I'm mortal after all," I had written in an email to my family last year when I told them about the diagnosis. I was very glad not to have an illness which was debilitating or which would hasten my death, obviously. But the conclusive diagnosis of an incurable and fatal disease was sobering. I had nothing like the trauma faced by people such as Stephen Hawking who had to deal with ALS (Lou Gehrig's Disease), for example, but I developed a more serious perspective on the universal condition of us mortals. By contrast, the rude shock of my pain and surgery last year had been a very brief experience, reflected upon mostly after the issue had passed.

Early one evening I came upon a trail maintenance crew, vigorously repairing trail tread and clearing encroaching brush. The crew was organized by the PCT Association, together with the Forest Service. I stopped to tell them how much I appreciated the work they did, benefitting this trail, a national treasure, and in particular benefitting me and other hikers. A young man in the crew looked up abruptly when I mentioned that my trail name was Over the Hill Jim. "I hiked with you!" he exclaimed. It turned out that he was Eric, the young man I hiked with for a while after Rock Star left the trail in Oregon last year. It was the end of the crew's work day, so I stopped to visit and to eat my dinner with them. Then I moved on to complete my hike for the day.

On Wednesday night I arrived well after 10:00 pm at Cold Spring Creek where I planned to camp, tired and hiking by the light of my headlamp. This was not fun. I needed water, but I couldn't find anything in the creek but muddy puddles too shallow to pump water from or to scoop it out. Late as it was, I could hear loudly partying campers in the nearby campground beside a road. Preferring to avoid car campers, I walked a little farther until the noise subsided behind a small ridge and then made camp. I ate the energy bars for my next day's breakfast and went to sleep. Next morning I arose in quiet daylight and soon found plenty of water I could filter. I prepared a breakfast of the dinner intended for the night before, and I feasted.

While I was eating I noticed a large tree stump almost waist high that was on the other side of the trail before me and in front of a Forest Service tool shed. Sitting on the stump was a whiskey bottle, less than half full. I mused that the partying car campers must have left the bottle for the benefit of PCT hikers. Sure enough, a solo hiker soon came along and stopped when he saw the bottle. He did not notice me sitting on the other side of the trail, as he was transfixed by the sight of the whiskey bottle. I watched as he walked over to the stump and examined the bottle, sniffing its contents. He pulled out his one liter bottle, poured out a little water and added some whiskey. He tasted his spiked water and was evidently satisfied, for he replaced the whiskey bottle and put his water bottle back in his pack. I was sitting only 40 or 50 feet away from the guy, so I thought it best not to move or make a sound so as not to startle him. He walked on, unaware.

I smiled at the sight of the hiker spiking his water, but I was not tempted. At times I could have enjoyed a dash of whiskey, but not right after breakfast. Besides, I was unsure what effect a little alcohol might have on me while hiking, and I surely did not need any help to relax when I stopped.

I was not enjoying hiking at this pace anymore, so I decided to revise my hike plan, aiming for 12 – 14 mile days in place of 15 – 17 miles. I speculated that my need for a slower pace might be due to an increased need for oxygen, so that now I was affected by the thinner air even at an altitude of just 6,000 or 7,000 ft. Or perhaps last year's surgery somehow accelerated my decline and cost me a little stamina. Or did I simply fail to train enough? In any case, I was not trying for a speed record, an endurance test, or punishment. Slowing down required some accommodation, that's all. I wasn't going to burn out or to quit.

When I next called Zhita on the sat phone I had decided to meet her a little sooner than I originally planned. I finished this section's hike ignominiously on Thursday, after walking down a dirt road to paved Highway 96 and waiting there for my ride. I was five miles short of the end of this section of the PCT and my goal for the week. I felt a little guilty about meeting Zhita before I finished the section, but hiking the last five miles into Seiad Valley on a paved road was not the kind of experience I signed up for. I also was glad to save some time by meeting her before rather than after those five miles, as it was already late afternoon. Someday I hope the trail here can be routed through the wild country which far better suits the hiking experience.

Zhita did not see me sitting by the road when she first drove by, but she turned around and drove back until she spotted me waving my arms. I settled for seeing the last of this section of the "trail" from the seat of the car. The forest in Seiad Valley was a fine setting, and I relished the sight of the Klamath River. We got out of the car to look at the torrent of water, and I was glad to be able to cross the river on a bridge. I had read that the cost of building a bridge over that river was a major obstacle to rerouting the trail here. Getting the trail off of the road will require construction of a very substantial bridge to safely support hikers and horses and also withstand the onslaught of water each spring when the snow melts. This is another weak spot in the long, thin line of the PCT.

Tired now from just five days of routine hiking for a little more than 70 miles, I remarked on the contrast with the beginning of my hike the previous year when I had set out from Seiad Valley to hike a gain of 4,500 ft. in pretty warm weather on the first day with no particular difficulty that I recalled.

2009 Zhita

This is The Year After.... After the dramatic—and traumatic—experiences that interrupted the trek in 2008, my beloved, with his always spirited self, is ready to get back on the trail. He has planned for this segment to begin on August 1, so, once again, he makes his elaborate preparations.

I, on the other hand, am in a frenzy with one of my many community commitments. This time it's the Residents Association for our apartment community, of which I am a current Board member. There is a political stew going on about the way that former officers had handled association funds. One of our new officers is a lawyer, and he is probing deeply. Accusations fly and emotions soar. A good time to leave—if I can leave all this behind; but I know that emails will follow and the Responsibility Crown of Thorns seems forever fastened to my head.

But it is July 30, Jim is ready, and we are leaving tomorrow. And it is also Thursday, the day that my granddaughter Maya gets out of school camp early. So I go to Long Beach to pick up Maya, check on a day camp that she will be attending in the following weeks, then rush home to pack.

On Friday everything is packed, including all the papers, folders and laptop, and we are on our way! What a great relief to be on the road. … I love to drive, and there is a feeling of freedom in being, at least for the moment, disconnected from everything except the passing scene, the music on the radio, and each other. This time our first stop will be in the Bay Area where we have two daughters and where we will spend the night. Wonderful hugs and yummy pizza with daughter Kirsten in San Rafael.

The next morning, Wendy, Greg and Zhita Lynne join us for breakfast—food for us, but not for the Chisholms who are fasting. More hugs, lots of teasing (always). Lovely time. We also meet Chris, a great guy friend of Kirsten (who eventually becomes a player in the PCT adventure). But we must get on the road again for our next rendezvous with more family– Jim's cousin Chuck and his wife Bev live in Oroville. They are a remarkable couple whom we seldom see so there is lots of chatter over lunch and more hugs before we are back on the road on our way to Yreka to spend the night.

One of the things that I love is food. Good food in good company is one of life's little treasures. And little treasures so enrich my life. So I head to the Black Bear Diner with Jim for good food with my best companion. This PCT adventure has opportunities for such highlights.

But Saturday morning, August 1, brings us back to the realities and the uncertainties of this year's PCT hike. As we drive to the trail, hug and say goodbye, I think we both feel the drama.

How will Jim manage? What will be the unforeseen? Will he accomplish what he has set out to do?

I drive back to the motel in Yreka, and, reluctantly, check my email and participate in a conference call. More outrageous stuff going on with the Residents Association. But I am not there and that, for me, is a plus. I spend the rest of the day driving slowly around the little town, taking time to note the areas for future walks, shops to explore, places to eat, and I settle in.

The next evening, as I am in the motel working on my computer, I hear people talking about wildfires, apparently not in this area. However, during the night this stays with me. I wake at 2am and get very anxious about J. I turn on my cell phone and get up to read....

On Monday J calls about 8:30am. What a relief! He says he got quite tired yesterday but reached his intended destination. I will be so glad when this first week is over and he returns for hugs. I know that next week Susan Wanser will join him—not only a companion, but a nurse.

I have quite an accomplished day myself. I write lots of email, finish Section 7 of the online traffic school class that will help to lower our auto insurance rate. Then out for a walk in Greenhorn Park. I love discovering these special places. This one has a lake with blackberry bushes tucked into the periphery. I stroll, pick, and munch. What a delight!

Daughter Deb calls and we discuss Maya's not entirely satisfying day camp experience. Deb also says that, to her surprise, she has discovered lots of stuff about me online. (I suppose it's about professional publications I wrote and other stuff about my career in education—not very exciting but I guess we love to see the names of loved ones in print.) I go to Miner Street and browse in a book store and a thrift shop where I get some fun bargains—a charming mug with a whimsical little chicken strutting around its rim, a floppy hat, and a brightly colored blouse—all too cute and too cheap to leave. In the evening, I go out to purchase some greeting cards, then settle in the picnic area at Miners Inn to read and discover a Natalie Thai Restaurant for my evening meal.

Wednesday morning Jim calls very late to report that he is behind schedule and plans to shorten his distance tomorrow for pick-up…. I walk around town and discover the Community Garden. Wonderful place. As I stroll through, I meet a family of members who are checking on their plot. We stop to chat about the garden and its place in their lives…. Another treasure on my walk route is a metal sculpture gallery. I wander with eyes focused on the treasures. I guess my appreciation shows for I am always considered a potential buyer. Sorry to disappoint, so I smile, chat about the art and artists and continue on my way. At Greenhorn Park, I find the old mill and mining equipment—history just standing there inviting musings about the past and the people who might have worked here. I know that Jim will also consider this a treasure so I take photos and add it to my list of experiences that I will share with him on his day off—if he has time after his clean-up, sack-out, re-pack, and all those other little essentials for the next leg of his hike.

Thursday: I wait anxiously for Jim's call. When it finally comes, he can't complete the conversation before his signal fails. So I stay in my room all day waiting for the next call. At 2pm, I finally decide that I have to get started toward the proposed meeting place. I put beer in the cooler—and J calls!! What a relief! The route is easy—no problem. Ironically, I am so focused on the road that I ride right past J, then turn around for a second try and see him waving his arms. Those wonderful arms that give the best hugs in the world.

On Friday we drive to Ann's—together. And we face another dilemma. This time it has nothing to do with the trail. Just the need for a transfer of funds from our money market account to our checking account. At home this would be so simple—we would just write a check on one account and deposit it to another. However, we have not brought checks for the money market account with us. We are able to connect with TIAA-CREF by phone, but nothing is simple. We have to get a "Medallion signature" in order to submit a phone or online transfer request. So we go to B of A for the Medallion signature, then to UPS where we pay $30 to mail it to TIAA-CREF! What a nuisance, but at least we are together to deal with the logistics. And life—and our adventures—continue. There is a lovely break for dinner with Ann at McMenamin's, a charming restaurant right on the river.

Back at Ann's J reviews his maps for directions we will need for tomorrow. "Lots of stress," I note. It is also gray and very cold, and I am chilled—not very helpful for my spirits.

Saturday is a sunny day!! Life always feels so much better, brighter, of course, that way. I drive J to the trail. Quite a challenge to find it, but at least we are together. Back at Ann's to find her sleeping off her fatigue and angst. I spend the day shopping and walking along the river….

Jim

On Saturday Zhita and I drove east and north to find Highway 22 and then Woodpecker Ridge near Mount Jefferson and little Pamelia Lake. We found the short trail back to the PCT near the scene of last year's rescue. I was kept busy with the map and searching for signs and landmarks while she drove, so Zhita and I were glad we could navigate the unfamiliar route together. After many hugs and my vow to stay out of mischief, I returned to the trail. There was less stone silt in Milk Creek this year, but it was easy to see where its name came from. Soon I gazed on the pond and my old campsite, scene of my rescue last year. It looked so ordinary now. I took a few pictures without the distraction of ominous pain, then was startled to meet a husky hiker called Slim, who strikingly resembled Lakota John. It was a surprising coincidence. That night I camped at Breitenbush Lake, a year later than I had originally planned to arrive. How different it was to be there now, comfortably healed after last year's drama!

Susan had decided to join me in this area to begin hiking together. She arranged to be dropped off at Woodpecker Ridge Trail the day before I arrived so she could start out by hiking alone a couple of days with less mileage than was on the hike plan I had sent her. On Sunday I found a note she left on the trail for me, a scrap of map paper peeking out from under a rock. She was continuing to hike ahead and would meet me later in the day. She noted that I picked the better day to start, as she got pretty wet and cold on Friday while I was still in town. A northbound hiker then overtook me, and I asked him to take a message to a woman named Susan ahead of us, letting her know that Jim had joined the trail and was on the way.

In this area the PCT lies a little within the western boundary of the Warm Springs Indian Reservation. I turned onto an appealing dirt road for a short distance east into the reservation to eat my lunch. The scenery was much more enjoyable there, where an open meadow allowed me to see farther than the trees surrounding me. Soon after I sat down to eat, a car with two Native Americans drove up and stopped beside me. One of the men asked where I was coming from and where I was going. I realized that he might be concerned about hikers camping on reservation land and leaving litter behind, so I assured him that I was there only to enjoy the scenery while I had lunch. I had a schedule to keep, so I would be returning to the PCT very soon. He seemed satisfied with my answer and drove on. I smiled at the irony that it was Native Americans who traversed this forest in a car, while city folks walked.

After lunch I found another note on the trail saying Susan got my message. Later in the afternoon I found yet another note saying she was doing well and still moving, probably going on to the next spring. I made camp another night without catching up. Next morning I was sure we were close, but after hiking for nearly two hours I decided I had somehow passed by her campsite. At 8:30 I left a note for her saying I was going back as far as the power lines to look for her. But I did not find her, so I turned around again and started back. I put my own note in my pocket with her notes (no litter) as I continued. I found Susan just a quarter of a mile beyond where I had turned back! Now we would hike together. It became clear that she was at least as strong a hiker as I was and well able to match my pace.

Susan is a very adventurous person, having been an instructor with Outward Bound for two years earlier in her career, and she had paddled her kayak in a month-long group outing along the coast of Alaska. Now she had decided to hike with me for two weeks rather than just a few days. Her friends thought she was crazy to set out on this long PCT hike with a stranger, but bold action was not unprecedented for her. I supposed she judged that I was harmless enough, and I had enough experience now to come up with a reasonable hike plan. And Susan loved hiking. Zhita and our daughters were all glad that I was going to be hiking with a nurse. Susan had pointed out that her specialty was assisting with baby deliveries, a skill I was unlikely to need, but her general knowledge and experience was reassuring.

Zhita

On Sunday, J calls at 8:05! Wonderful! He sounds good; is two miles behind but thinks he can catch up today. Ann seems to have stomach flu; sits in her chair all day. I spend much of the day writing columns for the Residents Association Newsletter. But I do take a break to go for another long river walk. So restorative.... By evening, Ann is feeling better and asks to hear about my projects. I tell her about the Residents Association and the League of Women Voters intern program.

The next day, J calls with a change of plans. He has discovered that the altitude is too hard on his lungs, so we will meet a day earlier and regroup. Remarkably, he used the word "enjoy".... Imagine that?

Ann and I go to her son, Randy's, to pick up some crabs that he has caught. I go shopping and talk to daughters Deb and Wen. Wendy and her family will be going to LA, then to Tijuana for some kind of mission project. In the evening, Ann, her friend Jane (mother of Ann's daughter-in-law Amy) and I go back to Randy's for a dinner of crab cakes. Delicious food, and quite a cast of characters....

On Tuesday, J's morning call voice sounds good; he is on schedule and has met up with Susan. I have a working day, busy with my usual LA projects. Wendy calls from Long Beach where she and family are hanging out in the pool at Deb's. They all sound good. And Ann is peaceful....

Wednesday, the 12th is an interesting day. The TIAA CREF saga winds down: The letter has arrived and phone access to our account is arranged! I go to Trader Joe's for Jim's beer, then pack and get on my way to meet him and Susan. We meet at the lodge and drive Susan to the campground where she will spend the night. The weather was cold and rainy, not very hospitable. We eat goodies that I have brought; then Jim and I drive to Hood River where we are staying in what proves to be a great motel. After cleaning up and unwinding, we get to a restaurant at about 9:30. Good food always welcome.

Jim

On Tuesday one of the people we met was Crop Duster, walking 40 miles this day so he could be at Timberline Lodge for their famous brunch next morning. Susan and I reached Timberline Lodge at 5:30 on Wednesday the 12th, having hiked 71 miles, and Zhita arrived at 7:30. We took Susan to the nearby campground where she had decided to spend the day off. Since she would not be hiking before we rejoined her, she left her trekking poles in the car. Zhita and I drove on to a Hood River restaurant at 9:30, then to a motel.

I spent much of the next day revising my next week's hike plan to include less ambitious 12 to 14 mile days, continuing the pace I had found

I could enjoy this year. But now I feared I would not be able to hike 10 mile days in the much higher altitude of the Sierras anymore, so I reluctantly called John and Kirsten to cancel our plans for a September hike. John told me that he was glad to find out when he did, because he was not enjoying his strenuous training for hiking in the Sierras. Kirsten was just disappointed and more than a little concerned about my continued hiking.

On Friday morning Susan called Zhita on her cell phone to ask us to pick her up at the Timberline Lodge rather than the campground. When we arrived, she had all her gear spread out to dry in a conference room, barely tolerated by some annoyed staff of the lodge. She told us she had forgotten that her trekking poles were key to erecting her shelter, so it was very difficult to keep dry without them. She did not call us earlier to ask us to return from Hood River to bring her poles, because she did not want to interrupt our time together. We chided her for not asking for such a simple favor! Susan and I finally started hiking at about 11:00, in the chill fog and rain at a temperature of 37 degrees as Zhita noted.

Zhita

I stay for a tour of the historic Timberline Lodge, originally built during the Great Depression by the WPA and beautifully done. I drive down the mountain and back to Ann's. She is coping with family concerns and feels very depressed. So I fix dinner for the two of us—and wish I had a magic wand...

Saturday—I guess just the wish for the magic wand worked. Ann wakes very up-beat, and we spend a lovely day together. We drive to the Oregon Garden in Silverton.

On Sunday Ann's amazing landlady and friend, Aletha, comes up in the morning to chat. She has just had surgery to remove skin cancer from her nose. Aletha is also a wonderful gardener with an amazing garden of which there is a full view from Ann's window. Much pleasure for me.... Ann and I spend the day together. We drive about 20 miles to Cottage Grove, a resort with more lovely gardens—and a theater where we see Into the Woods, a take-off on Little Red Riding Hood. Delightful!

Back at Ann's home, Susan's partner, Jayneese, comes to pick up some of Susan's stuff that I brought back for her. We sit and visit—very pleasurable.

On Monday Ann and I go shopping for a fountain for her patio. Sounds like a lovely idea, but we give up early on when Ann thinks about the maintenance involved. And today Jim calls on his cell phone (rather than his satellite phone)! He is in range of civilization. He has reached Cascade Locks; that means he is at the border between Oregon and Washington. Another state has been trod!

Jim

Somewhere in the mountains after we had reached Lolo Pass, Susan and I were descending steep switchbacks into a ravine dense with aspens. Susan was a few yards ahead of me as I followed the trail swerving left past a large fallen tree. There was a sudden commotion right behind me, and we both whirled around to see what was making the racket. We could only guess that it was a bear, startled from its nap very close to the trail, for the unseen creature charged through the trees up the steep slope to get away from us. Surely only a bear could thrash like that straight up the mountainside, violently shaking the slender trees! "Wow" I said, softly, "that was pretty close."

For the last part of our hike in northern Oregon I had elected to take the famously popular Eagle Creek Trail as an alternative to the less scenic section of the PCT. That proved to be an excellent choice. Eagle Creek was a delight to see as it crashed precipitously down the gorge, often in the form of waterfalls. We took pictures of each other at the entrance to the tunnel which takes the trail behind a 150 ft. waterfall, an often-photographed site. I was glad that neither of us was afraid of heights, for parts of Eagle Creek Trail were very narrow, blasted out of the sheer rock wall of the gorge far above the turbulent creek. We both made use of the occasional pieces of cable anchored to the wall of the gorge to provide a handhold. Horses could not walk on such a narrow trail with the overhanging rock close above, and I wondered if some hikers turned back as well.

After we reached Interstate 84 along the Columbia River bank we followed a connector trail east to rejoin the PCT. Along this section, near the highway but below the sight and sounds of it, Susan was a little ahead of me. In a small clearing among the aspens she called out, "Jim, look, a bear!" I hurried a few steps into the clearing, but all I saw was a cluster of thin aspens vigorously quaking their green leaves. I missed seeing the bear, but once again I did not regret that the bear charged away from us.

On Monday Susan and I reached Cascade Locks with its wonderful view of the Columbia River and a very pleasant, grassy campground. I could even call Zhita on my cell phone that evening and again the next morning. When Zhita's daughter Debbie learned that I was reachable on cell phone, she called to say hello. (Zhita said that Debbie later told her that she had called me to check up on my rendezvous. I presume she was reassured that my voice did not sound evasive. Susan was hiking with me for adventure, not romance.)

We hiked across Bridge of the Gods over the Columbia River, leaving Oregon to enter Washington on Tuesday morning. There was no pedestrian lane on the bridge, and the only car that passed by gave us a wide berth. This was the lowest point I would hike on the PCT, at an elevation of only 200 ft. With some reluctance I had changed my plan to follow the guide book's suggested alternative route before us along paved Highway 14 rather than the official trail which climbs and descends a lot in the coming section with little to offer in water or scenery. The highway was more direct than the PCT, saving some of the time lost at my slower pace, but walking on the edge of a paved road was still not what I signed up for. The irony did not escape me that I had rationalized riding in the car over five miles of paved road leading to Seiad Valley, and now I had chosen to walk a paved road route in preference to a standard if unappealing trail tread. Oh well, I had long since abandoned any illusion that my PCT hike would be perfect.

The best compensation for my choice of route was in the bountiful ripe blackberries along the highway. I had never tasted such delicious blackberries! Susan loved them so much that she hated to interrupt eating blackberries in order to continue walking. And soon the road took us through the village of Stevenson, where we couldn't resist stopping for another treat. Susan enjoyed a milkshake, and I had an extra breakfast which Susan recalls as artery-clogging. Such luxuries we indulge only on a long hike.

After we turned off of the highway to climb up Panther Creek Road, we came upon a wonderful garden in the very large yard of a home beside the road. The garden was filled with vegetables. The owner of the garden turned out to be a trail angel, for she gave us water for our bottles and some of her fresh tomatoes and corn. We climbed on up from the river to reach Panther Creek Campground, my revised destination for the week. Zhita joined us at 1:00 pm on Wednesday, and we all set off for Hood River. There we waited with Susan for the arrival of her partner Jaynese and their daughter Shelby. Susan had hiked 155 miles with me, and she didn't even seem tired.

After our new friends departed, Zhita and I welcomed the comforts of our motel and the restaurants in Hood River. I finished revising my hike plan by noon on Thursday, pleased that the shorter distances each day allowed me to enjoy hiking as much as I had in previous years. New reality accommodated.

Zhita

8/19 Very hot day.... J calls at 8am. He reached the campground last evening, and I will meet him today. I load the car with all the stuff he will need for resupply and for our day off together and leave at about 8:45. Close to my destination, I am confronted with yet another search. I can't find the exact dirt road that leads to Panther Creek. Signage would really help, especially if you could see it from the road. Sigh…. But I find it and am greatly relieved—until I am in the campground—and try to find #16…. When I finally reach J at about 1pm, I am once again elated to see him and Susan. The three of us drive to Hood River where we meet Jayneese and their daughter Shelby. Having completed her segment of this year's hike, Susan goes off with them.

J and I go back to our haunts in Hood River where we will stay for another day. It is, as usual, a time for taking deep breaths, drinking toasts as we clink our wine glasses, eating great food, and taking in this great adventure. I note that the temperature is 102 degrees….

8/20   A day off the trail. During dinner at Brian's Pourhouse, we decided to declare today a "Friday." For us, Fridays have always been special. When we were working, we established a Friday Night ritual. That began in 1983 with the very first Friday that we lived together. Coming home from work and looking forward to the weekend together, we began the evening by sitting on the couch in our living room, sipping Manhattans, and nibbling hors d'oeuvres, and just enjoying time to relax. This was such a pleasure—and we had so many hors d'oeuvres—that the dinner that I was prepared to serve seemed superfluous, so we skipped it. But, for me, no festive repast is complete without dessert, so, of course, we had dessert at our place on the couch. This was such a pleasure that Friday Night has become a special tradition. On Friday night, we make no plans for movies, theater, parties…. Just the two of us and Manhattans, hors d'oeuvres and dessert. So, at the restaurant, we ordered Manhattans, hors d'oeuvres, and dessert. Although it was Thursday for the folks around us, it was Friday for us.

On Friday Jim is ready to get back to the trail. He is really looking forward to hiking alone for the last week of this year's hike. We drive to Panther Creek, hug and say good-bye, and Jim sends me off—in the wrong direction. ☺

Jim

I had really enjoyed hiking with Susan and getting to know her, but now I looked forward to hiking alone again for my last week on this section of the trail. I had continued to find that while it was more fun to hike with a good companion, I prized the experience of hiking alone.

Zhita and I returned to Panther Creek Campground on Friday. I set out heading north for a gain of almost 4,000 ft. the first day with no special difficulty. But on Monday when I hiked up to an elevation of 6,000 ft. on the side of Mt. Adams, I felt dizzy and seemed to see the trail swaying from side to side momentarily. Perhaps I now needed to slow my pace going uphill, a caution about hiking in the Sierras. Otherwise I was fine.

I found a small box on a post holding Wilderness Use Permit forms for Goat Rocks Wilderness, so I filled out a form for my last two days of the hike. In the evening I met an Americorps crew in the midst of a ten month assignment of trail maintenance. I thanked them heartily for the work they were doing to preserve the scenic treasure of the PCT. The crew leader urged me to join them for dinner, for they had more than enough. I was glad to have something novel for my hot meal in such a social setting, so I stayed with them a little longer.

I continued doing well, and I reached the next meeting place a day earlier than planned. Thanks to the sat phone, Zhita was prepared for my early arrival. As I neared Road 5603 where we would meet on Tuesday, I came to the wonderful clear water gushing from Lava Spring. I was only a mile and a half from the end of my hike for the year. I would have given a lot to find such a bountiful spring in countless other areas of the trail! I scooped up some water in my bottle and drank it, unfiltered, just to see if it was as good as it looked. It was.

I had hiked about 345 miles closer to my goal. All was well.

Zhita

The next day I drive to Portland to visit my cousin Deborah. This is a special opportunity to visit with a relative whom I seldom see otherwise.

Deborah is much younger than me, and she was raised in Texas, far from the rest of our large New York based family; but we have discovered that we are kindred spirits who both value our family relationship.

We spend two days together, sharing stories about our lives and families, ways we are alike, our religious background. And we eat well, visit interesting places like the famous Chinese Garden and the local café, bakery... just exploring the neighborhood as we chat and eat.

8/25   Another day of drama trying to find Jim on the trail. Left Portland at noon; sailed through to Randle, then onto the forest roads. I soon realize that I don't have enough information. I pull off the road and into the community of Cispus Central with no idea of what I might find. Hoping for knowledgeable people, I am delighted to come upon a Forest Service office. A personable ranger gets out a Forest Service map of the area and proceeds to search. He decides that the way Jim has advised won't work, so he plots another circuitous route. I get back in the car, riding slowly on the unmarked dirt roads. I turn on the GPS in the car and find it very comforting. Amazing that it knows where I am even when I am on dirt roads.

I finally get to J at 5pm; he has been waiting since 3. But he is cheerful and eager to show me one of nature's treasures—the huckleberry bushes—so that I can pick and eat. Reminds me of the days of my youth when I would pick wild berries in the fields and forests in New York and New Jersey—although I remember the berries of my youth as being much more succulent. ☺

On our way back, I realize that the ranger had sent me in the most round-about way; the PCT map, which we followed on our return, was much shorter and a much better road. Live and learn....

8/26   Today we pack up and drive to Springfield where we will stay at Ann's. After tending to some housekeeping at Ann's the next day, we leave about 10 and drive to Medford where we will meet Gary Stevens, a very nice guy whom Jim met on the trail last year, the fateful year of the kinked intestine. In fact, it was Gary who after having met Jim on the trail in 2008, prior to his kinked-intestine drama, when he saw the article about Jim's rescue in the local newspaper, called the hospital to find out if this was the "Over the Hill Jim" guy that he had met. I was pleased to meet him now and to get a chance to know this man and get a sense of the empathy that had motivated him to connect with us.

Back on the road, we drive to Williams to spend the night in California.

8/28 We spend an enjoyable day, first visiting the history museum in the old high school, then driving on to San Rafael to visit with daughter Kirsten. Kirsten is getting ready to move from San Rafael to San Anselmo so we go with her to get some boxes, pack up some of her books and other stuff and drive to her new apartment. Very nice place in a lovely area. We go out to dinner together, then visit with K's friends, Brent and Stacey. Life is good.... But there are a few bumps in the road: Daughter Debra calls to talk about some problems she is having with her mortgage and "hot flashes," a new complication in her life. And the motel in Williams calls to say that I have left my briefcase.... We will have to return.

8/29 Deb calls to say that she is feeling much better today. After breakfast in San Anselmo, we and K drive to San Francisco and browse along the waterfront till noon when daughter Wendy and family arrive to meet us for lunch. The highlight of the day is a ride on a Duck Tour. We have a marvelous driver-guide, spirited, caring and an amazing joie de vivre. Lots of laughs, bumps and fascinating scenery. We all go back to our motel where granddaughter Z is delighted to take a swim in the pool. With all of us piling into our motel room, we laugh and joke over pizza and salad. Zhita, sometimes quiet and shy, is warm and uninhibited. Splendid day!

8/30 And today we head for home—on a circuitous route that takes us back to Williams to pick up the briefcase (a great relief)—then on to LA. We had left the Bay Area at 8:30am and arrived home at 6pm. J sorts the mail—no surprises. We walk to a neighborhood Chinese restaurant for dinner, then settle in for life at home.

Jim Back to the Sierras

I needed to find out how my newly reduced capacity for miles of hiking each day at lower altitudes might affect my mileage while hiking at higher altitudes. Sobered by my slower pace this year, I did not want to tackle the skipped Sierra segment with other hikers until I knew what I could do. I rented a bear canister again, this time a small one. I drove alone to Florence Lake on Wednesday, September 2, well after snowmelt. After picking up my wilderness permit at the Ranger Station in Prather along the way, I made camp in Jackass Meadow Campground. I tried day hiking the next day and had no difficulty getting enough oxygen, going up the steep, rugged Dutch Lake Trail for a gain of 1,700 ft. to an 8,800 ft. elevation. I was pleased to find that I managed the day hike okay.

Friday morning I bought a round trip ticket for the ferry and took the 8:30 ride across Florence Lake. I then hiked more than seven miles carrying a stuffed pack which must have weighed 50 lb. to climb about 1,500 ft. to an 8,890 ft. elevation, again with no unusual trouble breathing. Unfortunately, I saw no wildflowers at this season. I made a dry camp –no problem with snow now. I noted that I needed to repair my tent's vertical screen zipper.

On Saturday I hiked north over Selden Pass with almost a 2,000 ft. gain and then back to my campsite carrying about 40 lbs. I was reassured to find I could still hike 10 mile days with my pack at altitudes of 8,000 to about 11,000 ft., though I was slow going uphill. Now I was sorry I had canceled this year's plan to hike across the Sierras, but I would have hated to have Kirsten and John and our friends set out on a major hike with me into such remote country only to be forced to turn back because I could not handle it. Perhaps my poor performance when I began this year's hike in August was simply due to not being adequately conditioned? Now I seemed to be back in the condition I was in last year.

I hiked back to the lake and the ferry on Sunday and then drove home. While on the boat crossing the lake I was riding with a group on a Sierra Club hike which was a pretty ambitious outing for working people on a brief vacation. One of the hikers was incredulous to learn that I was playing chess by satellite phone as I hiked.

Gene and I traditionally played chess by email, making one or two moves each day. It was his idea to try it by sat phone while I was on the PCT, calling each other once a day as we were able to and leaving a voice message with the next move. I enjoyed the novelty, though I didn't play very well.

I had hiked about 20 miles with my pack, but my PCT miles here didn't count toward my goal because I had already seen this part of the trail.

2010 Welcome?

This would be the big year, the year I planned to hike the final 400 miles through Washington to reach Canada and essentially complete my quest to hike the Pacific Crest Trail! Darbi, Sawyer, Tanner and friends planned to hike with Grandpa on this final portion of the trail, Kirsten planned to hike with me for the last section, and Susan planned to hike with me for the last several sections. Gene would hike with me from Snowqualmie Pass for a day hike. Zhita would meet me each week for the whole trek. I was sure to have a wonderful hike this year even if some of the plans were not realized, but best of all would be stepping over that Canadian border, at last.

In my preparations for this year's hike, I had discovered that the Canadian government now required a permit to enter the country on the PCT where there was no customs or immigration office at the border. The deadline for applying for a permit this year was in June, and I first learned about it in July. The consequence was that instead of finishing the PCT with an extra seven mile hike to Manning Park and a paved Canadian highway, Kirsten, Susan and I would have to turn around at the border and hike back an extra 29 miles to the nearest US road at Hart's Pass. Zhita would meet us there.

Assured that August is the best (driest) month for hiking in Washington, Zhita and I reached Packwood on Sunday, August 1. I picked up my wilderness permit for my group of hikers at the ranger station. The next morning we retraced our route on the more direct roads back to the trail where I had left off the previous year. Among the huckleberry bushes once again, I struck out to the north.

Soon I was hiking in Goat Rocks Wilderness, a spectacularly scenic area. Hiking at a comfortable pace, I found these rugged mountains to be one of my favorite sections of the trail. The alpine terrain offered views of peaks, ridges and canyons I could only dream of when I hiked through the dense forest at lower elevations. On the other hand, I was also exposed to the wind and to rain or snow. Tuesday evening I hiked a short side route down to Bypass Camp, shielded from the wind as the guidebook promised. No storm materialized that night, but the sheltered basin was welcome.

The next day I made my way on crunchy old snow up to a narrow ridge from which I looked down into a deep canyon, with frozen Goat Lake visible in the distance. The direction of the trail from here was not clear, for an untrodden snowfield stretched out on the slope before me. I puzzled over the course to take. Continuing in a fairly straight line seemed a likely route for the trail, while ascending an unmarked and rough steep trail up the rocky ridge to my right offered a route avoiding the snowfield. I studied the guidebook's description of the scene, finally identifying the Packwood Glacier before me. The book warned that sliding down that glacier was risky.

I had no ice axe, of course, and I could only guess where the trail might continue on the far side of the snowfield. How much of that snow was resting on ice, and how treacherous was it likely to be? If I had seen a set of footprints successfully crossing the snowfield, I might have assumed the hiker knew where the trail was on the other side and followed those tracks. Now, unwilling to risk sliding out of control down the glacier before me, I chose the safer alternative route and clambered up the steep rocky ridge.

Snow was patchy on the rugged ridge route, and before long I came to a trail junction. I noticed a new-looking sign uprooted and lying face down on the ground. I discovered that the sign had pointed to the PCT hiker's route continuing up the ridge and to the stock route to the left, a trail blasted directly across the rocky ridge well above the snowfield. Apparently that untrodden snow blanketing the glacier was not where the trail went at all. The hiker's route continuing up the ridge turned out to be longer, steeper and very rugged, and it had been judged unsafe for horses. The stock route looked shorter and easier to walk on but with less of a view of the Goat Rocks Mountains.

I puzzled about the sturdy new sign as I propped it against rocks so it could be seen. I could not imagine how heavy snow or rock falls could have gotten the sign post out of the rocky ground. Hiking the extra distance and climbing up an extra 500 ft. of elevation on the hiker's route turned out to be well worth the trouble for me, for the views were spectacular.

To my surprise, high along this rugged part of the trail I met a man on horseback with a pack horse in tow. He was a cheerful, outgoing man who was glad to talk about his trip on this section of the PCT. He told me where he had been and a little about how he handled his horses. He lived in Washington, and he had traversed sections of the PCT on horseback many times. He clearly loved the Washington outdoors and the trails he rode in the wild land. I enjoyed his enthusiasm for riding the PCT.

However, as he went on to talk about his previous treks, the man described an unfortunate experience from the year before. He was traveling alone with two horses on a section of the PCT farther north. When he saw an inviting little glen below the trail with a pond and grass, he decided to make camp there. The steep terrain did not offer many such campsites for equestrians. When he came to a side trail leading down to that glen, it was posted with a sign saying "No Stock." Indignant at being told he could not go there, he told me, he knocked the sign down and threw it away. He then proceeded down that side trail. Unfortunately he lost his pack horse off of the steep little trail. He explained that on difficult trails he can handle very well the horse he is riding, but it is much harder to manage a pack horse following behind. He really regretted losing his horse, but he was undeterred by that one bad experience. He simply rode more carefully now when he took a pack horse on the trail.

Later I thought to myself, "That man is crazy! After an experience like that, having killed his pack horse by taking it on a trail marked unsafe for horses, here he is now with two horses on another hazardous trail that was identified as unsafe for horses." I have no experience with such riding, of course, so I am not familiar with the issues he faced. Still, I was pretty skeptical about this maverick's judgment.

Then I thought of the sturdy new sign which I had found uprooted and lying face down off the trail – where it could not be read by a person on horseback. The maverick? He may resent such signs telling him he can't go where he wants to, but other equestrians might appreciate the information such signs offered. I doubt that the Forest Service has a trail maintenance budget adequate for keeping in place their cautionary signs about stock on this part of the PCT. The man did not appear to be older than 50, so he may be riding this trail for years to come.

On Thursday I reached Highway 12 at White Pass. As I descended the switchbacks down to the crowded parking area beside the road, I was hailed by a man who asked if I would like a beer. It was early in the day for that, but I decided to join him on the tailgate of his pickup where we enjoyed a near-lunchtime beer. I had been planning to take a break anyway. The man was a backpacker who hiked a week at a time on trails in the area, so we talked about some of our experiences. He was scouting places where he might hike next. When he saw me walking down with a backpack he decided it was time for a beer, a spontaneous trail angel opportunity. "One beer is plenty for me, thanks," I assured him when he offered another. We wished each other well after our brief visit, and I crossed the road to continue on my way. With a beer in my belly and only two days till I met Zhita for a day off, I didn't need to trudge down to the nearby store as I had intended.

The trail continued through rugged country. I came to Highway 410 at Chinook Pass Saturday afternoon. As I descended to the road, I spotted Zhita down below talking to a group of day hikers just arriving at the parking area. I waved and got the attention of some other hikers still descending the switchbacks, and I called to them to tell her I would be right there. When she got the message, she looked up and waved. It was wonderful to be reunited, as always. We returned to Packwood late Saturday for a busy day off the next day.

Zhita

What a summer this has been! Daughter Debra's long anticipated—and, in spite of medical reality, hopefully to be avoided—heart valve replacement surgery has finally come.

(Background: In 1983, the year Jim and I married, Debra, my always healthy athlete daughter, became ill. What was diagnosed and dismissed initially as the flu, brought continuing misery, and led eventually to the accurate diagnosis of bacterial endocarditis. After weeks in the hospital, during which she became a shockingly weak invalid, and months of medical follow-up including research by my brother, Howard, a career scientist at NIH, it was determined that Deb would need a heart valve replacement. Faced with the decision about whether to get an animal or mechanical valve, Deb, who was eager to have children, had opted for the safety, but much shorter life, of the animal valve. She was told that the valve would probably have to be replaced within two to 10 years. Sounded very scary to me, but she was an adult, and I knew that the decision had to be hers. The valve lasted almost 30 years, but now it was done....)

The surgery took place in July and was declared very successful. After a few days in the hospital, Deb returned home. Understandably, she needed lots of support. Coping with the always mysterious after-effects of such a complex surgery brought times of misery and angst. I wanted to be there for her—and I was. When Jim's hike time came, she assured me that she would be okay. Would I be able to leave? I wasn't sure—until the last moment when things seemed to be going well. On July 29, I took her to the doctor for a blood test, then to the supermarket to buy dog food and family food. I picked up granddaughter Maya from day camp and took her and a friend to the Aquarium for birthday fun.

Deb and I talked some more, then I went home for a late dinner with J; I finished my packing and prepared for the road. What a wild week this has been! But I guess we are going....

The next morning, we started on the road to the PCT. I have qualms but I am glad we are on our way. We drove to San Anselmo to see daughter Kirsten in her new apartment; she has lovely things everywhere. We have good food and good conversation. K seems to be in a good place.

After breakfast, we are on our way again. While on the road, I talk with Deb several times. At the end of the day, we have a long talk during which she expresses her anger about people expecting her to be happy and charming when she is dealing with such dramatic changes. She talks about having time to think about her life. I consider this a very important conversation; glad that she is reflecting.... And then her day includes wonderful surprises. Many of her best friends come to visit and to celebrate Maya's birthday. They bring all the party stuff with them. Wayne and his cigar friends join the celebration. Deb is transformed.

Greatly relieved, I am ready to continue with the PCT mission. We drive to Springfield, meet Susan Wanser for lunch and reminiscence, then drive on to Packwood. After a night's rest, we are ready to return to the trail —to the place that I had such trouble finding last year. But this time we are together—so much easier. But so hard to let him go.... I drive back to the motel, organize stuff, and search for a motel where J and I can stay for the weekend when everywhere is full. I take a brisk walk to town and back—3 miles, one hour. Not bad.... Deb's evening call comes with a happy voice. She is doing well. What a relief!

Wakening the next day, I feel very lonesome; I so miss J, Deb, Maya, Wen, Z. There are no calls, so I do small errands and continue reading Light in August; really enjoying it. I wander out, find the post office and library, drive to Morton, walk, eat dinner, and then drive back to Packwood.

On the following day I drive to Yakima in the eastern part of Washington, just as a side adventure. It is very hot. I see lots of empty restaurants, but eat in a quaint place tucked into a converted box car located near the old train station. I really miss California food. Guess there's no reason to stay in Yakima....

Back in Packwood, I walk some more and have one of those serendipity experiences. Strolling through a meadow of dried grasses, I see two young boys who have set up a little stand in the middle of the field. They seem to be selling something, so I stroll over to investigate and am tickled by their ingenuity. They have created little ghosts out of paper which they have twisted into amorphous shapes and used a pencil to add haunting eyes. Just right for Halloween décor and so whimsical I can't resist. Pleased with my purchase, I walk to the wonderful ice cream store and treat myself to an ice cream cone—my always essential dessert.

Today I have a special treat. Now that I'm in this part of the country, I take advantage of the opportunity to connect with my much younger and seldom seen cousin Deborah. We go to Mt. St. Helens to spend a spectacular day. Since Deborah grew up in Texas and I in New York in the days before air travel – or in my family, any kind of long distance travel – she and I did not connect until we were adults. But she is a delightful person, and I am delighted to have some time with her.

It is hard to imagine the remarkable event of the eruption of this volcano in the very recent past. In fact, I remember that J, when he was working as a marine electrician, had actually flown to see the aftermath of the eruption days after the event. Less dramatic now, but very beautiful in its own way.

In the evening, the family checks in—J is doing well; Deb has gone to the cardiologist who says she is doing well (she sounds good—very good); Wen is busy but sounds great; she and Z will be going to Nicaragua on a mission trip next week.

And then it's moving day again. I load everything into the car to move to Chateau Timberline. Check email, home phone, make calls, and talk to Deb. She is driving; sounds good. In the afternoon I go to a museum in town—quite interesting—then walk in the area.

For the next leg of J's trek, Darbi and the grandsons and their friend Melissa and her family will join him, so I stop at the camp ground in town to check on leaving Darbi's and Melissa's cars when they are on the trail. Everyone here is so friendly and cordial. I drive to Randall and south, looking for a road from which to view Mt. St. Helens, but I miss it.

On pickup day I meet J at Chinook Pass. There are the usual uncertainties: Right road? Right bridge? Right parking lot? But this time I stop to ask some folks. Jim spots me, calls to some other hikers to tell me he will be right there. So good to see him; I missed him so...

On this week's day off, there will be lots going on. Darbi, Sawyer and Tanner arrive, and we are happy and amazed. Sawyer, age 15, is now much taller than I am, with a deep voice and a face marked with teen allergies. Tanner, age 12, is still the little guy, but an emerging teen. They stay to themselves and read. Melissa and her daughter Olivia and Melissa's friend Mary Ann arrive. We all visit at the camp ground, a lovely gathering of folks but with no time for partying. J spends much of the day repacking, checking on his satellite phone voice mails and eating lots. We also go down the road to locate the essential Laundromat.

On hike day we breakfast with Darbi, Sawyer and Tanner at Peters Inn. Then I drive the clan to Chinook Pass. It takes two separate trips to get them all there. I feel like a taxi driver (before I ever heard about Uber). Alone again, I return to Crest Trail Lodge at about 2pm and spend the rest of the day catching up on email, correspondence, reading....

Jim

After the hectic day off and our joyful reunion with family and friends, Zhita ferried all of us and our packs to Chinook Pass, making two crowded trips in the Prius to get all of us there. The pedestrian bridge over the highway was now closed for repairs, so we started on the north side of the road. We headed north on the trail for a couple of miles to Sheep Lake. There we set up camp beside the little lake and explored the area, while a cold wind blew through the basin holding the lake. The Albuquerque and Tucson folks were chilled, but the altitude at 6,000 ft. was not a problem for any of us. Next morning we set out on a day hike for them, for they would hike with me until lunchtime and then hike back to Sheep Lake for another night. They would return to Chinook Pass and Zhita's shuttle service on Wednesday.

The abundant Bear Grass was in bloom, as well as Columbine and many other wildflowers. Mary Ann taught us the names of many lovely plants along the trail. But there was more adventure than we bargained for on our second day. Long-legged Sawyer strode on ahead of the rest of us; when Darbi and I came to a trail junction, we puzzled over Sawyer's apparent scuffed mark on the trail. We decided he must have taken the wrong trail, going left instead of right. We left our packs with the others and hurried ahead, searching and calling.

At last it became clear that Sawyer's size 14 boots had not stepped on the marshy part of trail where we were now searching, so we turned back. When we reached the fateful junction where the others had been waiting for about three hours, we learned that a couple of southbound hikers had told our crew that they had seen Sawyer on the PCT, patiently passing the time until we might appear. We were the ones who made the mistake, but we learned that only after an anguished search for him on the wrong trail. With great relief we hurried up the PCT to be reunited.

We rejoiced to be together again, which seemed a little mystifying to Sawyer. Then with hugs all round, I said goodbye and started north toward Canada. I now realized that it was important to plan for the possibility that, when hiking with others, we might sometimes become separated. I needed better ways to communicate with co-hikers who got ahead or behind in order to ensure that such a stressful and potentially dangerous situation did not happen again.

When I called Zhita on the sat phone the next morning, I talked longer than usual to explain what had happened. I felt badly about Darbi's needless anguish due to our misunderstanding of Sawyer's partially obliterated arrow on the trail, and I wanted Zhita to reassure everyone that the responsibility was mine, not Sawyer's.

Darbi and company hiked back to Sheep Lake without further incident, spent another night there and then returned to Chinook Pass to meet Zhita. After shuttling back to our motel room in Packwood, they cleaned up before making their way back to Portland. Compared with the drama of 2008 when Darbi and Kirsten had come to Oregon to hike with me and found me in a hospital instead, this year's hike was pretty successful. Darbi, Sawyer, Tanner and our friends had actually hiked with me on the PCT, and all were well.

Later that day I came to an opening in the trees which allowed me to see the trail stretching across an open slope ahead for a quarter of a mile before leading into the forest again. A white spot caught my eye, and I discovered that ahead of me was a wild goat walking north on the PCT. I managed to get a snapshot before the goat turned from watching me and ambled off into the woods. As I approached the trees I saw that his footprints were quite clear on the trail. The rounded front of his prints was quite different from the familiar pointed prints left by deer. I supposed that was because goats frequently leap from rocks to make their way in the mountains, especially in the Goat Rocks Wilderness behind me. Pointed hooves serve deer well in their customary manner of travel, walking, running or bounding on dirt and rocky soil, but such hooves would handicap an animal needing to spring off of rocks very often. Now I realized that Olivia had been right when she asked me earlier in the day whether what she was pointing to were goat prints on the trail. I hadn't recognized them. I took a picture of these goat prints to send her later along with the picture of the goat.

Zhita

I wake thinking about Deb and the complexities of her life, her values, the realities—and then, by contrast, the details and complexities of the arrangements for my meeting with J on the trail in Stehekin. Stehekin is easy—just a matter of calculation and adjustment. Deb is in quite another place. How can I be loving, honest, and helpful without compromising or jeopardizing our relationship? How can I be both parent and friend? I remember Dad's words: "You have the right to make your own decisions as long as you are willing and able to take responsibility for them." I have made so many mistakes and foolish decisions in my life, but I accepted the consequences and dealt with them on my own terms. Now Deb and I must both allow her to do the same. (My head feels like it is being squeezed by a cap of electrical tension; my feet the same. I guess it is a sign of confronting reality; pretty amusing....)

On the way to Randle I drive into camp ground to do laundry. Then I drive to Windy Ridge to view Spirit Lake. I am treated to views of Mt. St. Helens all along the way. I also listen to Cry the Beloved Country on CD, a revisit of a literary piece that holds up well. Back in Packwood, I walk on Route 12 and stop to take photos of a quaint firehouse to share with Wayne, my fireman son-in-law. In the evening, I watch a great program on TV (a very unusual activity for me), about Edward O. Wilson, a scientist who studies ants and applies his observations to sociology.

And then it is time for the taxi to get in gear again. I make the trips to pick up Darbi, Melissa, et al. They all seem to be in good shape and happy. After showers in my motel room, they are off to Windy Ridge. I have my long-awaited pizza—one of my favorite foods—go for a walk in Packwood on both sides of Highway 12, and have one of my coveted ice cream cones. Joys can be found in every corner...

And then I have a strange and slightly off day. On my drive from Packwood to Bellevue, I stop to see Pioneer Farm—a very interesting site that recreates history in the area. However, the motel in which I am staying is in the midst of freeway exits and a shopping mall, not the setting I had hoped for. I also realize that I have a urinary tract infection (UTI). Yuk! I spend the day doing errands and napping; don't feel like exploring....

But the next day is much brighter. Cranberry juice helped the UTI, and a Kaiser nurse phoned a prescription to the local Rite Aid. So I continue exploring the territory. I go to the Doll History Museum in Bellvue. Fascinating. Just sorry my daughters and granddaughters are not with me.

Moving day again. J due at the Pass at 2, so I decide to stay in Bellevue till noon. I ask at the motel desk about a bookstore that would not require my going through that crazy freeway intersection. The woman sends me off four miles down the street in the opposite direction, and I discover a beautiful area—trees, parks—splendid; and a great shopping mall. Buy some books, then back to the motel for lunch of leftovers. Then on to find the Dear One at Snoqualamie Pass. Incredibly, our meeting place is almost directly opposite the inn. We eat, relax, and exult in each other's nearness.

Jim

I reached well-marked Snoqualmie Pass on Saturday, August 14, where Zhita was waiting for me. I had hiked 70 miles from Chinook Pass, in addition to the 72 miles in the week before that. Our motel was just a few minutes' drive from where I found Zhita. It was a delight to be together again and to receive her assurance that Darbi, Sawyer and company were all well and in good spirits when they left Packwood to return home.

Gene had called Zhita to tell her that something had come up and he could not meet us here for a hike as he had planned. Brother John had called to talk about his recent whitewater rafting trip with former high school chums who had lured him into Montana this year instead of returning to the PCT. On Sunday I hurried to repack my food and supplies – amid lots of phone calls from family and friends checking up on me – so we could drive down to Cle Elum to scout out a detour from the PCT.

Here I had decided to make the most of the luxury of Zhita's support on my hike. A portion of the PCT ahead was closed due to bridge reconstruction work as well as other wildfire damage repairs. I had read that the detour was fairly extensive, involving both added miles and elevation changes which were not part of the PCT. Checking online for updated info about trail conditions was very helpful. What irked me was the piece of the detour which required walking on a paved road for several miles. I wanted Zhita to meet me after I hiked down to that road, drive me the few miles on the road and then let me out to continue hiking the detour. This way I would hike about the same number of miles on the detour as I would have if the PCT were open. It would be a frivolous indulgence.

Zhita noted that we spent three hours locating the road, the Mineral Creek Trail descending to it from the PCT and then the Pete Lake Trail which ascended back up to the PCT. We also verified that she would have no difficulty driving to these trails in the Prius on paved roads. We were fortunate in being able to explore the route together beforehand, for we had limited information about the detour and a sketchy map of roads in the unfamiliar area.

Zhita

The next day, after breakfast in our room, I take J to the trail head at Snoqualamie Pass—a 5-minute drive!—then return to the motel to do laundry, pack up and drive to Cle Elum. Get a lovely room, organize, then spend the day doing household errands—shopping, gas, Forest Service—and exploring a bit. Terrible dinner at a supposedly Thai restaurant. When the day cools off a bit, I walk in town, then back to arrange for a motel in Seattle. Miss J but will see him tomorrow. Check on Deb and relieved to hear that she is sounding good. Buy a real newspaper!

The following day, I drive to meet J at the trail detour. So wonderful that we had done a trial ride on Sunday. Everything works out just right. I try to do some sightseeing in Cle Elum, but most places are closed. However, I manage to get into the Telephone Museum—small but very interesting. I drive out to the train depot (closed), fish hatchery (no sign of life), eat at a pleasant Mexican restaurant.

The next morning, as I sat down to wait for J's daily call, it occurred to me that one of the advantages of this hiking partner role is that I have lots of time to reflect. Before I had a chance to write a single word, the phone rang. I rushed to hear J's voice but apparently the signal vanished. At least I knew he was continuing his routine....

Jim

On Monday Zhita returned me to Snoqualmie Pass. I hiked up onto the crest of the mountains, gaining more than 3,000 ft., to camp near Park Lakes. It was a long day for me, and I went to bed after just a snack, certainly not my preferred dinner. Early next morning I quickly reached the junction with the Mineral Creek Trail, prominently marked as the beginning of the detour. The PCT was closed due to fire damage. I turned right and soon began plunging down the sometimes heavily overgrown Mineral Creek Trail. I was glad to be going downhill as I fought my way through the alder saplings and brush. The trail ended in the valley at the road where I met Zhita, as planned. We were very glad we had explored her route and located our meeting site beforehand. We drove to the Pete Lake Trail which completed the detour by ascending back up to the PCT. I was famished, so before I started hiking, I prepared what should have been my dinner the night before and ate that as a hearty brunch. Zhita was amused to see how I "cook" on the trail, and she took pictures to document the little scene.

Zhita

It's moving day again, but after packing up I walk to Cle Elum for a last little adventure. I stop at the Craftsman shop, see beautiful stuff, buy some cards. I eat lunch in the motel room, then leave to go on to Seattle. Although the motel there is in a slightly seedy area, I have a very pleasant room. When I ask at the desk about things to do in the area, the staff directs me to Green Lake. Gorgeous place! Lots of folks walking, running, boating. I walk a 3-mile route around the lake in 45 minutes. Legs and back surprisingly sore; take a pill and keep going.

The next morning J's call introduces a new dilemma. The road to Harts Pass where I will meet him next is very rough and we know that is a problem for our low-slung Prius. I will need to find a solution... But that's a couple of days away, so I continue my own exploring. I spend an interesting day wandering around Pike's Place, an amazing market area. Flowers, one of my passions, are gorgeous—and cheap. The market guys toss fish to bystanders; there are remarkable street performers everywhere. I walk to Pioneer Square; stop at the Art Museum—impressive building, very savvy security guard—a woman artist! At the square, I see guys playing chess with huge pieces on a board laid out on the ground. I stop at the Klondike Gold Museum. Taking buses to and fro, I meet remarkably nice drivers, both men and women.

(Throughout the day, I have had intermittent feelings of faintness, mild pains in my chest. While I am concerned, I keep going, and seem to snap out of it. I wonder if I still have that UTI—or need more water— or ate something wrong...?)

Life is about solving problems; one of the joys of life is solving problems. Today I solved the transportation to Hart's Pass problem, and, as usual, a responsive person was the key to the solution. The guy who answered the phone at the North Cascades Base Camp in Mazama was the kind of guy who says a thoughtful "maybe" rather than a routine "not what we do." I can hardly wait to tell J! Yesterday I found Agua Mira, and today I found out about a shuttle to Harts Pass!

(I start reading Faulkner's <u>Light in August</u>. What a pleasure to unravel the threads....)

Then I drive to meet Susan Wanser, who will hike the next section of trail with J. We make a very pleasant drive to Stevens Pass where we find J waiting! How wonderful! Susan starts hiking, and J and I drive to Leavenworth, a quaint town, where we stay in a quaint motel. I take a breath and unwind....

Jim

When I had hiked back up to the mercifully lower elevation of the PCT, at the junction with the Lemah Meadows Trail, I met several hikers who had just walked through the closed section of the PCT! They said the repair crew was cleaning up and preparing to leave. The new bridge was in place, so the trail was passable in spite of the signs still telling hikers to take the detour. My little side adventure was unnecessary! After this I would be a little more skeptical about the requirement to follow detours. Having clambered back up to the PCT, I was met at once with another 2200 ft climb which the guidebook cautions is best done in the morning if the day is warm. It was a warm afternoon. Ah well, at least Zhita had given me a ride for those three miles of paved road below. Many other hikers must have hiked it all, unless they found their way through the closed section of the PCT.

On Friday I happened upon three young hikers taking a break. They were section hiking, and they had talked about hiking the whole PCT someday. One of the hikers was inspired to hear that after all my adventures I was aiming to reach Canada this year. I enjoyed his warm response to my brief account of my hike, including my rescue and recovery two years before. These young men hiked faster than I, so the enthusiastic hiker asked when I expected to reach Stevens Pass, my next resupply point and the destination of their hike. I expected to arrive at midday the next day, and he said he would look for me at the pass.

Sure enough, when I descended toward the lodge at Stevens Pass on Saturday, I saw someone walking toward me. It was the young hiker, there to greet me with congratulations and good wishes for the remainder of my hike. At his urging, I went with him into the lodge where we met his brother and friends. After a brief round of introductions and well-wishes, I joined them for a group picture.

I'm sorry that now I can't find my note with his name and email address. (I should have had a system for keeping my notes!) We have not been in touch since then. His warmth and enthusiasm were an inspiration to me as well, affirming my sense of accomplishment in hiking so far and urging me on to my goal.

I had hiked another 76 miles this week, doing fine at my subdued pace. Zhita arrived with Susan, whom she had brought up from where they met in Seattle. Susan started hiking right away to give her some extra time on the trail to settle into the routine before I joined her. She was a little concerned about whether she was in condition to match my pace, in spite of her experience the year before which had shown that she was easily able to keep up with me.

Zhita

On J's day of preparation, it is important that I not distract him, so I read as he packs. I am rewarded at meal time, when we have three good meals out, including dinner at the lovely Tumwater Inn, and ice cream cones on the way back to the motel. K calls early in the day with disappointment about her very reluctant decision not to join J on his trek. Her stamina is not secure. This is a sad but wise decision for her.

And then it's trail day, with beautiful weather and J in good spirits as I take him back to the trail. Then I focus on reservations for Stehekin. I call, but there is no phone response. Go to the library to use their computer. Voila! It's done! Spend time walking and driving the wooded areas of Leavenworth. Beautiful! With a river that runs through it all.

After some more exploration in Leavenworth, I am on the road again on the way to Wenatchee. In Cashmere, I discover another remarkable historic collection—a model village with Indian and pioneer dwellings and artifacts. I love to happen upon these places and just stroll to explore and learn more—places I would never have seen if it were not for my role as part of J's hiking adventure. In Wenatchee, I do my usual wandering to find the motel, post office, and just discover. And I am able to make arrangements to get across Lake Chelan to meet J at Stehekin.

On the following day, after taking care of the household financial stuff, I drive to the farmers market and roam the stands to look at all the wonderful stuff. I buy some cucumbers and corn and get free tokens to ride the trolley, which takes me on a full loop around Wenatchee and East Wenatchee. While the route is fairly dull, the trolley driver, a young woman, is very interesting. The rest of the day is taken with small errands, more wandering, and, in the evening, watching a documentary about New Orleans and Hurricane Katrina.

Next day I write some reflections in my journal, exercise, then go out to Ohme Gardens. What an amazing place! Very rugged walking, almost entirely steps. With my uneven legs, awkward gait and poor balance, I do as much as I dare and make a mental note that this is a place I must revisit with J. In the afternoon, I remember that there is a park area near the river. I drive over, then walk through a gorgeous and well maintained area along the river. I see some of the remarkable sculptures that are located throughout the city. These are numbered and described in a brochure that I have picked up on one of my wanderings and I would like to find each of them. By evening, I realize that my legs and feet ache, so I sit in a warm bath—then, ironically, watch TV programs about wild hiking areas—Devils Staircase in Oregon and the English Channel Islands....

Today J's call does not come until about noon. He reports that he and Susan are doing okay, but Susan needs more stuff for the cold wet weather. I also manage to get in more interesting sight-seeing. The Wenatchee Museum has exhibits on pioneer living and an elaborate model train panorama to show the remarkable tunnel routes and terrain of the area. And I walk to see more of the items on my list of Avenue Sculptures. This is a city that appreciates its history and culture and I find that exhilarating. I wind up my day watching a TV program on female judges—Ruth Bader Ginsburg and the Canadian Chief Justice—interviewed by Nina Totenburg. (I realize that, for most people, watching tv is certainly not something to be documented; however, those who know me will probably agree that, for me, it is an amazing phenomenon. I guess I must have thought it was noteworthy as I included the details in my journal. ☺)

Finally I do the complicated packing and loading for Chelan and Stehekin. On the way to Chelan, I stop at the Rocky Reach Dam and spend much time reading the material about this remarkable place and its environs. At Chelan, I check into the motel then go down to the boat landing in preparation for tomorrow's boat ride. When all is settled, I wander through town, checking out restaurants, then shopping at Safeway to buy the Golden Delicious apples that Susan has requested.

Jim

After Susan left, Zhita and I were delighted to have a day off together. Hugs and showers and food and sleep, so luxurious after my days on the trail! I thoroughly enjoyed hiking in the mountains, but I also thoroughly enjoyed my brief weekly respites. We drove to Leavenworth and stayed in a quaint motel in the quaint town. The town is modeled after a Bavarian village, and we had a wonderful German dinner at Café Crista.

The next day Kirsten called very regretfully with her decision to not hike with me on the last section of the trail. Her stamina was not up to par, and she did not want to risk running out of steam in the wilderness. I was sorry she did not feel up to it now, but I agreed with her decision. She hated to miss hiking with me to the Canadian border. I was sorry to miss hiking together for that, and I was also sorry she would not get to know Susan on this hike.

I set out in good weather and good spirits from Stevens Pass the next morning. Susan kept up a good pace ahead of me, so I actually caught up with her only after hiking for two days. She left a couple of notes on bushes for me and sent a message with some southbound hikers, and we finally met at Lake Sally Ann.

Soon it became clear that the cold, rainy weather called for additional clothing for her. I wore my usual cold weather gear: long underwear in addition to long nylon pants and polyester shirt and my rain suit. As needed and at night I added a fleece pullover and a knit watchcap under the rainsuit. I slept in the next day's clean socks plus as much of my clothing as I needed. I seem to be endowed with a more tolerant thermostat than most, so I am mercifully a little less sensitive to changes in temperature. When I called Zhita on Friday I asked her to retrieve Susan's additional warm clothing from the bag of supplies she had left in our car and bring those items to Stehekin.

I had read online about an extensive detour necessitated by an avalanche in 2003 which had wiped out a sturdy horse bridge over the Suiattle River. The bridge was being replaced at a point farther down the river so that it would not be wiped out again, and the PCT required rerouting to access the new bridge. I read that many hikers were continuing to follow the original trail instead of the detour, crossing the river without a bridge. I also read some complaints from other hikers who found difficulty with the temporary route and also with the new PCT tread being developed. After my recent experience with a detour, I was inclined to stay on the original trail, and I was encouraged by the experiences of others who did so. Susan was game.

Continuing on the original trail, we crossed several creeks and streams, stepping on rocks or logs or sometimes wading. Along the way we met a surprising southbound hiker, a hefty sixtyish man who did not appear to be in great shape for backpacking. He told us that he found a good log crossing the Suiattle River ahead of us. The log was just upriver from the trail, he said, but it was too long and narrow a log and too high above the river to safely walk across. He admonished us that the safe way to cross the river was to sit down astride the log and to scoot across with backpack straps unbuckled in case of a fall. He said the occasional stub of a broken limb on the log was awkward to scoot over, but it could be done with care.

When Susan and I approached the next large stream, she had been counting the crossings and said we had not yet reached the river. She reassured me that this crossing was not a big deal, for the big river was still ahead. There was a log over this stream which looked substantial enough to walk across, and the strong flow of water discouraged us from wading. Using my trekking poles to tap on each side of the log to keep my balance, I walked across with only slight misgivings while I was over the rushing water. Susan thought my crossing looked safe enough, and she did the same. On the other side we soon found signs marking the north end of the detour. We had just crossed the Suiattle River! We chuckled at the thought of the other hiker as he scooted on that long log with its jagged stubs.

For our next resupply, I wanted Zhita to have the experience of the 50 mile boat ride to and from Stehekin and a visit to this isolated village where the residents have rejected any road connections as well as any power or telephone or other communication wires to connect directly to the "outside" world. Daily ferry boat and barge service on the long lake is supplemented only by some local diesel generators and a few satellite dishes in the village. Construction materials, diesel fuel, food and other supplies all came in via barge and boat. Phone, TV and internet connections by satellite were possible for a few, but that was expensive and infrequently used. Visiting this community promised to be a unique experience along the PCT, and I was pleased that Zhita would get to enjoy it.

In Chelan Zhita had a little help from the boat crew in getting all our gear on board the express boat (the one taking only two hours to travel each way) to Stehekin. The boat was named Lady of the Lake. Lake Chelan is narrow but very deep, filling a gorge which has no outlet. The reliable rain and snowfall keep the lake at a consistent level, offset by evaporation. In some places the lake bottom reaches more than 300 ft. below sea level, far below the surface elevation of about 1,100 ft. Views from the boat of the mountains and forest along the gorge are wonderful.

When the afternoon bus arrived in the village, she was very pleased to see that Susan and I had managed to catch the bus at its stop not too far from the High Bridge Ranger Station to ride from near the PCT down to the village. It had been a long, cold and wet hike for Susan and for me, and we had been looking forward to our reunion and day off in this little community. We had elevation gains of 2,000 to 3,000 ft. each day except the last, when we descended 3,000 ft. It was Sunday, August 29, and Susan and I had hiked 98 miles.

Zhita

Another amazing day! Up early, pack bags, breakfast in room. Then down to the landing to take a boat to Stehekin—gorgeous! Interesting narration. Check in at lodge and get settled in room. Wander, then take the shuttle to Rainbow Falls. Gorgeous! Spectacular! On the way back, we stop at renowned bakery and at the old schoolhouse. Back at the lodge, I relax, rest my achy joints, read, then walk, look and photo this beautiful area. Then I go to meet J and Susan. Sooo glad to see that they made the bus. Sooo good to hold and hug the real J! The three of us have a delicious dinner at the lodge. Then J and I visit. Sooo wonderful!

The next day was a peaceful lovely day with J in Stehekin. We start to think about home and life after the PCT.

Jim

We also stopped by the Forest Service office to ask about Gary, a friend of Kirsten's who was working for the Forest Service here as a carpenter. We met Gary later in the café where we talked enthusiastically about our hike, my daughter, and life in Stehekin. When he learned that we were sightseeing, he immediately offered to let us borrow his pickup. We declined his generous offer, but we enjoyed talking with him, an energetic man who had a fulfilling life in this isolated community.

Zhita

Then came an interesting collage of a day. J gets ready to resume the hike, excited because this is the last leg! Breakfast at the lodge. Susan comes by our room to bring stuff, get boots. The three of us go down to the bus and they are on their way. I take my return boat trip across the lake. Back on land, I load the car and head for Winthrop, a long drive through lots of unpopulated landscape. Winthrop is in the middle of nowhere, and there is not much to it (so far). The motel is pleasant; there is a good market next door with bread from the La Brea Bakery, one of our LA neighborhood iconic culinary treasures! I look for restaurants. Not much, so far, but I stumble into a funny little pizza place with wonderful food! I sit next to a lovely local family.

In the morning, I start the day by watching a hot air balloon launch from the motel window. The slow, graceful ascension…. What an amazing and beautiful sight. Then drive the long road to meet J and Susan at Rainy Pass, a place with a most fitting name. They are soaked and freezing. We drive back about a mile to a sunny parking area that I have noted on my way up. While J and Susan do some unpacking and spread their wet things out on the bushes and ground to let them dry, I set up a picnic table for a yummy lunch.

A couple of bicyclists towing small trailers pedaled up to our table to ask if we happened to have extra drinking water. I had brought plenty, of course, and we had an extra gallon for them. Bruce and Sue told us they were on a long trip from their home in Montana to California and beyond, a cross-country biking trip. It is very interesting to talk to them. We exchange contact information in hopes of connecting with them when they rode through the LA area later in the season. J and Susan resume their hike, and I drive back to Winthrop, stopping at a lookout point near Mazama. Back at the motel, I spread out J's wet tent on the motel lawn. I read, go to a Mexican restaurant, then talk to K who is feeling down about her health and spoiled plans.

Jim

On Tuesday morning I was excited about getting back to the trail, because this was the final stretch of the PCT. Canada was calling! Susan and I took advantage of the luxury of Zhita's support by carrying only a day's food to start and arranging to meet her the next day at Rainy

Pass to pick up the rest of our food for this last week. As it turned out, the benefit to us hikers was not so trivial, because when we arrived at the road we were cold and wet again. I realized later that, while we had hiked only about 20 miles from our bus stop outside Stehekin, our support team negotiated the 50 mile ride on Our Lady of the Lake and then a 103 mile road drive to join us. But she was warmer and drier in the boat, the car and the motel along the way.

After our brief picnic and drying-out time with Zhita, Susan and I were back on the trail. On the following day we saw a curious entourage approaching us on the trail; it was hard to figure out what we were looking at until they drew near. It turned out to be a young woman hiking with her two llamas and three goats, each laden with baggage! She was an artist, she told us, and she was going to her studio – any appealing scene where she could set up camp for a few days and paint landscapes. The llamas carried her easel, brushes and other large equipment, and the goats carried smaller items. She offered a delightful variation from the usual hikers we had met.

Thursday brought another interesting scene. On a long traverse of open slopes covered with huckleberry bushes and dry grasses, we spotted a dark object on the slope not far below us. It was a large black bear, busily gorging itself with huckleberries in preparation for hibernating. The bear spotted us and another hiker approaching from the north, so it simply tumbled down a little lower on the slope and resumed eating. We watched for several minutes as I took pictures, musing about how that massive animal could possibly consume enough little huckleberries to build up a layer of fat for its winter fuel. At last I had seen a bear in the wild along the PCT!

On Friday we stopped for a break in a sunny spot, and we were startled to see a fire department ambulance on a forest road above us, driving quietly but with red lights flashing. We mused about the sorts of emergency which might bring the ambulance into the woods on a forest road, and also the good fortune of the person needing rescue where an ambulance could drive in to help. On Saturday we stopped for a break at the ranger station at Hart's Pass to visit briefly with the Forest Ranger, who was standing outside the station. When I mentioned the ambulance we had seen, he seemed quite surprised, even incredulous, for he was usually notified about any 911 calls for help in his district. Perhaps we had seen a practice drive, maintaining the crew's familiarity with the forest roads.

As we hiked in this final section of the PCT we met some hikers who said they were planning to hike into Canada to Manning Park without having a permit to enter the country. They told us they knew of others who had done so with no problem. We also met a few hikers who said they applied for permission to enter Canada just two weeks before their hike, well after the official June deadline, and they received their entry permits with no difficulty.

I had carried my passport card with me in spite of having no entry permit (I was even legal for hiking in Arizona!), but Zhita and Susan left their passports at home. Without passports for all we could not take advantage of our newly discovered clandestine opportunity to hike in to Canada, for we could not reenter the US on a highway without the identification required by our government. We would follow my original plan, turning around at the border and hiking back 29 miles to Hart's Pass to meet Zhita.

We were making our way one dry but chilly day, cold enough to make me think I should soon slip on my rain jacket to block the wind. We came upon a couple of hikers who appeared to be about retirement age, and it was the man whose appearance was striking. He carried a substantial backpack like his wife's, but he was dressed in unusual hiking attire for the season. Besides his boots and socks he wore only a tank top shirt made of thin white fabric perforated in a vertical design and a black Speedo swimsuit. The couple was from Canada, revisiting the US on a week's outing. The man appeared to be enjoying this hike more than his wife was, though she was dressed warmly against the chill. Later Susan chided me, saying that she was really disappointed that I did not take a picture of the man in his Speedo swimsuit. I do regret that I didn't capture that memorable sight.

Susan suggested that we advance our schedule slightly since I had planned a short day's hike to reach, and then start back from, the border. I agreed to her accelerated plan, saving a day by setting up camp early in the day at Hopkins Lake where I originally had planned to stay two nights and then simply pushing on with daypack loads to the Canadian border and back. Midafternoon on Sunday, September 5 we reached Canada, at last! We cheered in celebration.

It took a few minutes for it to sink in – I had hiked from Mexico to Canada! I had hiked 2,600 miles in a grand series of adventures and reached my challenging goal. I still had a piece of the trail to hike across the High Sierras, and I intended to do that, but I was essentially done. Victory!

I felt I had really earned this achievement, even as I appreciated that a lot of good fortune was essential to my success. The partnership and support of my wife were key to such a wonderful experience and were the envy of other hikers. My brother John had hiked hundreds of miles with me, and now my new friend Susan had as well. My daughters and grandsons and friends had enriched my experience by participating in Grandpa's odyssey, and I could never forget that the whole thing would have ended abruptly without the capable aid of rescuers and a medical team in 2008.

I was glad Susan was there to celebrate this day with me. To record our triumph we took pictures of each other at Monument 78 marking the border plus a picture of the sign welcoming travelers to Canada. There was no such sign on the US side. In fact, as I understood the situation, there was no legal way for any citizen or noncitizen to enter the country here. But the absence of a metal fence or wall to cut off access to the US where no immigration and customs guards could inspect intruders was in stark and pleasant contrast with the PCT trailhead at the border with Mexico. Here was a lovely scene, the lush dense forest simply opened to view by the corridor cut through the trees, leaving a wide strip of green grasses gracefully sweeping through the mountainous forest.

I had compromised with my original intentions at times, and I had repeatedly accepted the fact that I depended on many others to make my feat possible. I even accommodated to the fact that I was slowing down, hiking fewer daily and weekly miles as the years passed and my hair grew whiter. Zhita sometimes remarked that she was pleased to see that I could make that accommodation. She knew me well enough to not take for granted my accommodating to my new limitations. But I had achieved my goal!

Susan and I started back to return to the campsite where we had left our tents and most of the contents of our backpacks. It was on this return hike that I finally figured out why my pack was uncomfortable, even though it was so lightly loaded. I realized that I was leaning into the shoulder straps, walking in a posture I had recently developed, unknowingly. It seemed absurd that my shoulders were almost as sore from hiking with a very light load as they had become in the last few days with a full pack. I was tired, and my posture leaning into the shoulder straps was poorly suited to the task. I was gratified to find that standing more erect with my head and shoulders back quickly relieved the soreness. I would benefit from this hard-earned insight afterwards as I corrected my recent tendency to lean forward with fatigue.

The next day we found a clearing in the forest large enough to permit a satellite call to Zhita to tell her the news. No matter what happened now, I had hiked the PCT from Mexico to Canada, lacking only a 50 mile piece of the trail in the High Sierras. I was determined that I would see that stretch of trail yet, but I was essentially done, successful in hiking 2,600 miles. "There's glory for ya!" I thought, recalling a line from some comic character of long ago. It was cold and snowing lightly, but that did not dampen our spirits.

Zhita

Labor Day begins with J's triumphant call—he did it! Yesterday he and Susan reached his years-long destination at the Canadian border on the PCT. I call all the daughters. Then I take an outing to Twisp—walk in the area along the river. Delicious lunch and lovely atmosphere at the bakery. Drive circuitous routes back to Winthrop. Walk some more along the river. Write in my journal—the sense of peace this experience has brought. The past seven summers and a lot of the rest of our lives—especially J's–have been invested in achieving this wild goal that J set for himself on a whim in 2004. Since 2005, he and I have been partners in this venture. We have come to treasure this shared experience and to share in the joy of his remarkable accomplishment. Tomorrow I will meet the transporter in Mazama and ride with him up to Harts Pass to retrieve the trekkers. And then the celebration will begin....

But I have realized that this year's PCT experience has also been a unique turning point in my life. In anticipation of our seven weeks away from home, I had taken this as the logical ideal time to review my personal priorities—to confront my mortality. Some might consider this morbid; to me it is liberating. All those dreams of peace and creativity will be realized now or never. Rigid responsibility for the people and the causes can be morphed into a peaceful sense of responsibility to be the me that I've imagined. These weeks have been so peaceful. The time that I spent weaning various groups and projects of their reliance on me has melded with the distance from home and the completely different environments into a joyous calm. (Is that an oxymoron? ☺) I do not dread returning to the responsibilities of home; I look forward to creating the next stage of my life.

This peace encompasses my relationships with the worlds of family, friends, colleagues, and the always perceived individuals, groups and causes that "<u>need</u> me." It also, of course, enriches the wonderful partnership with my beloved. Daughters and grandkids—I'm ready to play, create, collaborate! At 75, I might agree with Jim's funny little quote that I am "too soon old," but hopefully I am not "too late smart." Today is the first day of the rest of my life....

Jim

On Tuesday we reached Hart's Pass again to wait for Zhita and the transporter. Susan and I had hiked about 180 miles together to the border, then 29 miles back to the pass. By the time the lumbering high-clearance four-wheel-drive van appeared, five other hikers were waiting with us. One hiker was a woman who had fallen on the trail. She thought she had broken her wrist, so she was especially eager to return to civilization. After sitting and standing there a couple of hours without walking, I could not stop shivering when the transporter arrived. Zhita embraced me to celebrate, and then she hustled us into the van to get warm. We were done. Now we could sit in the warm vehicle and simply ride a few miles down to Mazama where our Prius waited. Done!

Zhita

I start the day very conscious of just enjoying the world around me. It is 7:30am and I am sitting in the window of the motel in Winthrop. The sky is watercolor gray, a thin veil of mist hovering. I watch small birds cavort playfully in the air. A large bird, perhaps an owl or a hawk, is perched at the top of a lone and naked tree, not moving, just observing. I am eagerly awaiting Jim's final call from the trail. Today we will start the celebration of his magnificent accomplishment and triumph. I feel so peaceful.... And then I prepare for J's celebratory return.

Buy stuff to decorate the motel doors for the festive return. Then drive to the Mazama store to meet Scott, the transporter with whom I have arranged to meet J. We ride up the road to Harts Pass—pretty dicey, especially since it has been raining. We come up to rocks in the road that he has to get out and clear before continuing. Sure glad I realized that I should not drive this road in the Prius. When we arrive at the meeting place, J and Susan are waiting along with 5 other people. All are wet and cold. J, my always hot-bodied guy, is shivering. I am really concerned. When we get back to the motel, J gulps down the beer that I have brought and then conks out.... I take the satellite phone to the post office to send it back for the last time. Later in the evening, the three of us go to dinner at 3-Finger Jacks.

A day together! Breakfast at 3-Finger Jacks before we pack up and leave. Lots of conversation with Susan as we drive her to Seattle. We have become good friends. But then it is lovely to be just the two of us as we drive on to Olympia. Phone calls to lots of folks. We both keep exclaiming and marveling that we are now moving into the next stage of our lives. So happy to be us; so much love for each other. J exults in his footbath. Camping stuff drying all over the room. Quite a sight!

Then a day just for us! How welcome…and how fitting that this should also be Rosh Hashanah, the first day of the Jewish New Year. This really does feel like the beginning of a new era. We drive to a motel in Roseburg. On our way out to dinner, we find the Bank of America and then realize that we were in this town on one of our earlier adventures. We even eat at the same Applebee's.

Drive to Oroville to stay with J's cousins Chuck and Bev. They are very welcoming. Bev fixes dinner and her sister Toni and her husband join us. Chuck talks and talks and talks. He's a delightful and amazing guy.

Bev and Chuck's son Chris and his wife Amy join us for breakfast. We visit and then leave on our drive to San Rafael. K looks gorgeous; seems very happy. She fixes lunch for us. We walk to the community garden, the seminary and other parts of San Anselmo. J and K nap and I read. Then we go to Tiburon for dinner at Sam's, right on the water.

We spend a wonderful day with K. Glorious weather! We drive to Point Reyes Interpretive Center. Dramatic spherical display of globe with analysis of natural phenomena. We walk the path of the 1906 earthquake. Back at K's apartment, we read newspapers and prepare for the party. Wonderful gathering at K's for pizza party to celebrate J's accomplishment. K's friends Scott and Katrina, Brent and Stacey, Phil and Al, and Chris join us. K has made a picture on a card with staples removed from J's stomach after his surgery in 2008. Glorious time!

September 13, the great day of return! As we drive on our way home, we stop in San Francisco to meet Greg and Wendy, see their new apartment, visit, and tour the neighborhood. Then we're on our way. For me, it feels good to be returning and still feeling free. No weight of "Responsibility" ready to descend.... We stop at Harris Ranch for dinner. At home, we unload some stuff then have a mini "Friday Night," our special tradition of manhattans, appetizers and dessert. And then to bed. Lovely....

Transition from road to home. Formerly routine things seem less familiar. Cooking seems especially needing of reorientation. A pleasure to be back in the realm of Trader Joe.... J and I go through tons of mail, an interesting way to reconnect. Deb has her first day back at her job working with kids as an occupational therapist with LAUSD. She sounds great. I feel very peaceful. This really does feel like a new life.

Jim

The drive home was festive. We returned Susan to her car in Seattle, and we made celebratory stops to see Ann, Chuck and Bev, Kirsten, Wendy, Greg and young Zhita as we went. We celebrated some more when we arrived home. Zhita and I talked about our achieving a milestone which would mark a turning point in our lives. Much of our time and energies during each of the last seven years had been devoted to my hike. One short makeup hike remained for next year, but the organizing of our lives would now change substantially. We talked about new options and other projects for life in retirement.

I unpacked my hiking gear and supplies and, to save space in our apartment, put much of it in storage. Gradually we filed away notes and hike plans and guide books. Zhita, ever the librarian, organized much of that. She encouraged me to think about writing the story of my hike to give to our daughters and grandkids, but I was not ready to consider that. I was done.

Sequel

Lakota John was the young hiker my brother and I had met on the PCT in Oregon in 2008, who then showed up the following week to stay with me and keep the bears away while I was waiting to be rescued. Lakota John and I kept in touch occasionally after that. In the spring of 2011 I received a troubling phone call from him. Hiking south on the northern section of the PCT in Oregon, he was calling from Timberline Lodge on Mt. Hood. John had been stricken with abdominal pain and severe diarrhea, and he called to ask me whether I thought his symptoms were like mine on that fateful day in 2008. After describing what he was experiencing, he also asked whether I thought he might have either food poisoning or giardia. John said he had been careless about washing his cooking pot and also about filtering creek water, so either problem was possible. I did not dare try to say what his problem was, but I urged him to see a doctor right away. I feared that the problem was serious.

Later John told me he talked to a Forest Ranger he saw in the lodge who said he should hitch a ride to a nearby town to see a doctor. None was in residence at the lodge. Soon a doctor found that John had salmonella poisoning as well as e. coli! Both of John's unguarded mistakes had resulted in dire consequences. The doctor told John that he might not have survived if he had tried to tough it out on the trail. With medication and bed rest, alone in a motel room for the next two weeks, John's ghastly discomfort subsided, and he recovered. He later told me that the experience had taken the romance out of hiking for a while.

It was rare serendipity that two hikers who met by chance on the PCT subsequently each encountered a life-threatening crisis and that each in turn was able to offer some assistance to the other in his difficulty. Of course the best part is that each crisis was resolved with full recovery. We are alive! John continues to call me and Zhita from time to time, and he has adopted us as his "honorary grandparents."

2011 Finally

This year for sure I was determined to see those last 50 miles of the trail in the High Sierras which I had failed to hike before. The trail there went through a roadless wilderness area in central California, a little south of Yosemite. Gaining access to and from those 50 miles of PCT required a more than 80 mile hike at high altitude with no feasible resupply. I would be slow, but I was sure I could do it.

Kirsten was keen to make this hike with me, and we talked on the phone several times about her stamina this year. I felt that she would prove to be stronger than she gave herself credit for, and I encouraged her to commit to hiking with our very supportive group. With training and preparing, she rallied and became determined to hike with me. Susan had decided that she wanted to do this hike with me as well. Kirsten's friends Chris and Brent also decided to hike with us. My brother John was torn about the decision, but he finally decided he would not try it. Darbi could not afford to take the time off from work, and there was no access in this section for Gene to join me in a day hike. Harking back to an old truckers' song, I thought we would "have us a convoy," an unstoppable team which would surely be successful in our crossing of the High Sierras. Zhita was very pleased that I would not hike the Sierras alone this time.

Planning, preparing and training for the hike once again was the main focus of my life for a few months, though a trip to visit Darbi and family in New Mexico left me with less than ideal time for training. Having read about the record snow pack in the Sierras from the winter before (I did my homework this time), I decided that we should hike in September rather than August, a usually safe choice for section hiking in this area. We needed to wait longer than usual for the snow to melt and for the prolonged mosquito bloom during snow melt to subside.

As the time drew near, Brent found he could not take so much time off from work, so he decided he would hike in alone over Taboose Pass to meet us on the PCT. He would leave his car at the trailhead on Taboose Creek Road, north of Independence and Mt. Whitney, and then Zhita could return him to his car after she met us at Onion Valley.

As I had planned for my aborted attempt in 2009, we would drive to Florence Lake and then hike south and east on the PCT/Muir Trail to emerge over Kearsarge Pass and down to Onion Valley, near the town of Independence. We would not add a side trip to Mt. Whitney. Kirsten discovered that there was a shuttle service available from Fresno to traverse the rough road to Florence and Edison Lakes, so Zhita would not have to drive over that hazardous road. Susan would fly to LA, and then Zhita and I would drive with her to Fresno to pick up Kirsten and Chris at the Amtrak station. We would all drive together to the shuttle station, and Zhita would drive home on good paved roads. I planned that she would later drive to Independence and on up to Onion Valley to meet us at the end of our hike and to shuttle everyone to their routes back home.

I had considered myself successful in essentially hiking the PCT already, but I really wanted to see this final missing section of the trail. I was not such a perfectionist that I would fret over the few alternative routes I had taken along the way or a couple of short skipped pieces of the trail, but 50 miles in the Sierras was huge. I wanted to see that. And that nagging regret about my unfinished dissertation had arisen during my years on the PCT as a similarly major, self-chosen but unfinished goal. Achieving the final piece of my hiking goal should be cathartic.

I determined that we faced an eight and a half day hike at my high-altitude pace. We would ride to Florence Lake and stay one night in Jackass Meadow to begin acclimation to the altitude, then head out. On Friday, September 2, Kirsten, Chris, Susan and I clambered into the shuttle van in Fresno for our ride to Florence Lake, along with several day hikers who would also camp in Jackass Meadow for a few days. Zhita drove home. The shuttle stopped in Prather where I picked up our wilderness permit, and everyone who lacked a California fire permit completed the little chore. The scenery along the rough, precarious road seemed much more enjoyable while riding carefree with an experienced driver of the route. When we arrived at the lake we shouldered our packs and made our way to find our campsites. A short hike at 7,000 ft. seemed no problem to any of us.

The next morning we were all doing well at the altitude. We packed our gear and hiked back to the lake and its convenience store. We bought our one-way tickets for the boat ride across the lake and then made our way down to the dock where we boarded the boat. At the east end of the lake the boat was met by a man with two pack horses in addition to his saddle horse. I learned that some stuffed duffel bags on the boat were destined to resupply some hikers who would meet the loaded horses at Muir Trail Ranch near the PCT/John Muir Trail. (The two trails are the same in this section.) I asked the horseman about the service he was providing. It would cost the hikers several hundred dollars to resupply this way, convenient but pricey. The resupply opportunity extended only a few miles to the north or south from the ranch, limited to the distance the horses could travel from the ranch and return to it in one day.

We had a very modest five mile hike for our first day while acclimating to the High Sierra country, so we gleefully took time for a refreshing dip in the hot springs just south of the Florence Lake Trail. The weather was very mild, so we did not mind it when we emerged from the warm water to dry ourselves with our skimpy backpacking towels.

Each of us carried a lot of food for our long trek, and with the addition of the mandated bear-proof canister my pack once again weighed over 50 pounds. After dinner we still had some food which we could not fit into our canisters. We had to take our chances with the savvy bears in the area as we bagged and hung the surplus food from a tree, nearly conking Susan on the head in the process.

On Sunday we reached the trail junction where we entered the PCT/ Muir Trail. Soon we were surprised to hear a sound like cow bells. We found a father and son hiking with three alpacas carrying their packs. They told us they had rented only two animals, but when they started their hike the male let them know he thought he was loaded with too much weight. He laid down and stubbornly refused to budge. The owner of the animals then brought them another alpaca to share the load. The hikers were enjoying their luxurious outing, and they were pleased to stop and talk about their pack animals and to pose for pictures.

We walked by Wanda Lake, treading where I had slept in 2006 when I decided to turn back. Without the covering of ice and snow, I saw that the lake was larger than I had realized. Not hampered this year by deep snow, we made our way up to Muir Pass, at long last. Limited snow patches and our easy pace made hiking up to the 12,000 ft. pass no special challenge, just the expected huffing and puffing. We were amazed to see such a sturdy stone hut at the pass, erected long ago by the Sierra Club.

Looking ahead on the other side of the pass, I was finally seeing the rugged landscape which I had never seen. I was awed by the towering peaks and the cold, still valleys of the High Sierras. The formidable terrain through which we must somehow walk stretched out for miles before us. Could I really do that? There was a trail through it, but could I carry my pack all those miles in the thin air of this vast and forbidding land? No helicopters ventured to attempt rescues at this altitude, I had read somewhere. I took a deep breath.

We charged ahead. There were more snow patches and some snow fields still remaining on this slope, but they were not a problem. We could walk through the melting snow. We reached the bridge over the South Fork San Joaquin River ahead of schedule after gaining 1,100 ft., so we hiked on a couple of extra miles to camp near McClure Meadow. This hike was going well.

We hiked to Evolution Creek on Monday with a gain of almost 3,000 ft. to sleep at 11,400 ft. I admitted to difficulty hiking with my pack at this altitude. Kirsten urged me to share some of my load with the others, but I was not willing to compromise on that.

On Tuesday we reached the Bishop Pass Trail junction, near the Kings Canyon National Park's Le Conte Ranger Station, my landmark for looking for a campsite for the night. Brent joined us there, having hiked 20 miles north from the junction with the trail over Taboose Pass where he had entered the Sierras. We were delighted to meet up with so little difficulty apart from Brent's challenging solo hike up over the pass.

A little later we met the Park Ranger, and I told him how pleased we were to see that he and his crew had made it a priority to cut through the many recent blowdowns across the trail so that hikers could get through. He said that is always a priority when they return to the high country each spring. But this year was exceptional. Whereas they usually have to cut through about 35 downed trees in his jurisdiction, this year they found more than 300 trees sprawled across the trail. The previous winter's record heavy snowfall weighed down and broke almost all of the trees in some areas, and in a number of places on the steepest slopes we had observed the courses of avalanches which had downed every tree in their paths.

We heard that most hikers who had entered the High Sierras in June or July this year had turned back, unable to get through without snowshoes or skis. Later we read that even when the snow was melting, it was very arduous for hikers to try to forge a way around some of the sprawling tangles of fallen trees. We were glad the Park Service did so much work for us and also that we hiked so late in the season.

After we talked a bit, the ranger asked me if I would do him a favor and mail a bill payment for him. He spent the summer in the park, and the bill would be due before he reached a post office. I immediately agreed, appreciating so much the work he did to maintain the trail. When I stowed his envelope in my map pocket, he pulled a can of beer out of his jacket pocket for me. I protested that it was not necessary and he should keep it for himself, but he insisted that I take it. Our little group shared a taste we had not expected to enjoy for another week.

When we stopped for the night, we also shared the delightful treats of cheese and crackers and wine which Brent had carried in for us. It was a festive occasion.

During our trek through this National Park Wilderness area, I commented about the lack of signs at trail junctions where signs would have been helpful. In a previous year a Park Ranger had confirmed to me what I had heard from a few hikers, that the National Park Service had a policy about trail signs in wilderness areas which was different from the policy of the US Forest Service. While the Forest Service maintained a limited number of trail signs for the safety and convenience of hikers and equestrians, the Park Service had adopted a policy of not maintaining or replacing any such signs in wilderness areas. The Park Service policy was to promote a more pristine concept of wilderness, treating signs as intrusive marks of civilization out of keeping with its concept of wilderness. Old signs were tolerated as long as they were serviceable, but they were removed as they became damaged or illegible.

I took exception to this Park Service policy. As I understand it, the main reason for preserving wilderness areas is to permit people to enjoy the wilderness. It would not be appropriate for this purpose to, say, fence the areas off and prohibit anyone from entering them. It would be similarly inappropriate to decree that trails should not be maintained in wilderness areas because trails scar the landscape. Such a policy would restrict the enjoyment of wilderness experiences to elite hikers skilled at route finding. Far fewer people could enjoy the wilderness in comparative safety. Careful judgment is needed in deciding what is or is not allowed in these valuable areas, of course, but where there are trails for people to hike on, I think the safety offered by occasional trail signs far outweighs the visible impact of a few small signs.

Wednesday's hike included gains totaling 2,400 ft. to our camp site near Lower Palisade Lake at 10,600 ft. I felt a little nauseated, so I shared my dinner which I could not finish. Kirsten exclaimed about my fatigue, mild headache and not feeling well, my unusual lack of appetite and also my waking up gasping for air a couple of times during the night. "That sounds like altitude sickness!" She was right, but I protested that my symptoms were not acute. Besides, I would descend to lower elevation sooner by completing the hike than by turning back now. I was not going to be carried out again. Not if I could help it, anyway.

On Thursday we reached the Taboose Pass Trail junction, where Brent had come in to the PCT, surprisingly early in the day. Kirsten and Chris urged that we stop hiking for the day and camp here. The ranger had told us that a storm was forecast for tonight, and we could position our tents now to avoid puddles later. Chris said I should allow for a day off in the middle of such a strenuous hike in any case. Seeing that the party agreed, I accepted that. How appropriate it was became evident when I crawled into my tent and slept more than an hour. Kirsten, accustomed to my usual 15 or 20 minute naps, was worried, but I assured her that my long nap was very refreshing.

That evening I found that in my home-prepared dinner I had used too much Indian spice, so I could eat only half of it. It was too spicy for anyone else to eat, so Brent offered to carry the remaining half of the meal for me until we reached civilization and a trash can. At Kirsten's urging, I consented to let my friends carry a few other items from my pack as well.

On Friday we climbed nearly 1,400 ft. and descended more than 3,600 ft. I was reminded of what my brother would say whenever he was going downhill on the PCT, "What goes down must climb up!" I could tell that our new camp at 8,500 ft. was at an easier altitude for me, but the air still seemed thin. The next day we climbed a total of 3,500 ft. and camped at 10,700 on the Kearsarge Pass Trail, a little beyond the junction where we had left the PCT behind. None of us noticed the significance of our location.

Next morning I remarked that I had already completed the 50 mile missing link on the PCT! Kirsten exclaimed about reaching my goal without celebrating, so we cheered and raised our breakfast foods in a faux toast. Now we were on the Kearsarge Pass Trail, and tomorrow we would descend to civilization. While it helped that my companions were sharing some of my pack weight, probably reducing my load to a bit less than 40 pounds, I was fighting fatigue. But we were almost to the end. I would make it, I was sure.

Kirsten led the way, as usual, and at the pass (our fifth pass at about 12,000 ft.) she met Paul, a young man who had just hiked up to the pass for the scenery and the exercise. Paul would set out the next day on a solo cross country hike into the Sierras, so his little day hike up to the pass was a warmup for conditioning and acclimation to the altitude. When Kirsten told him about her 75 year old dad who was working hard to finish this hike to complete the PCT, he exclaimed that he would be glad to carry her dad's pack down to the Onion Valley parking lot where Zhita would meet us. When Susan and I caught up with our group, Kirsten exclaimed, "Dad! Paul has offered to carry your pack down to the car!"

I squinted up to see Paul silhouetted against the bright sky behind him. I hesitated. I had already completed my hike of the PCT, I rationalized. Now I was on a connecting trail which I had already hiked before. "Thanks, I would appreciate that." Kirsten cheered at my response. With relief I lowered my pack to the ground and unstrapped the lid from the main part of the pack. While the other hikers admired the view from the pass, I added water and snacks to the first aid and survival stuff already stowed in the lid. My little day pack was ready, with only about ten pounds to carry. I sat a few minutes more to catch my breath.

The scene before us was inspiring. We looked down from the High Sierras into sprawling Owens Valley with its flat farmland and occasional roadways stretching east to the distant, hazy mountains of Death Valley and on into Nevada. I had conquered the Sierras at last, and the slopes before me fell away to the promise of civilization below and my beloved wife. She was waiting just a few miles down there, and she had brought a car in which I could travel while sitting down! It was a wonderful prospect.

Now we began the final downhill stretch. Kirsten set the pace for the main party, following my "Sherpa" with my pack. Susan set the pace for me, a little slower than the rest but pushing the boundary of my comfort level. After all it was downhill, and it would soon be over. "Are you doing okay?' she asked frequently, looking back to check on me. Once again I appreciated the fact that my friend Susan, a nurse, was hiking with me – just in case. I was going to finish this hike if I had to crawl.

I made it. I was both exultant and exhausted when we reached the parking lot that afternoon and met my eagerly-waiting wife. It was Sunday, a triumphant 9/11 far different from some I remembered. Zhita exclaimed that I looked utterly spent, but I was walking on my own two feet. And now I had *really* completed the PCT. The old man did it! Hurray! Hugs all around.

Zhita had brought enough beer to share with my Sherpa Paul and our party. An appreciative Kirsten dubbed Paul "St. Paul of Kearsarge Pass." Brent and Kirsten got a ride to Brent's car from someone they met in the Onion Valley parking lot, and then they drove back to Independence to meet us at our motel. We all spent a night in Independence, with food, showers and rest. I was too exhausted to join the celebratory feast in the restaurant that evening, so Zhita brought a takeout meal to the motel room for me. She was concerned about me, but I insisted I was merely tired. Utterly.

Brent returned to the Bay Area with Kirsten and Chris the next day, and Zhita, Susan and I returned to LA for a couple of delightful days with Susan before she caught a plane home. All was well.

Zhita's Story

As I begin to write—rewrite—this section, I am feeling quite challenged. It is now August 2016, five years since this final segment of our collaborative PCT adventure, and my memory is blurry, even about the present, and certainly about the past. I had previously written my piece about this section of the hike some years ago, but it seems to have disappeared with the computer that we donated in 2015 during the chaotic move from our apartment in Los Angeles when our lives were upended with Jim's attack of West Nile virus…. So I will keep my mental fingers crossed and proceed to revive the images of the final triumph of the PCT finish.

Excitement, exuberance, holding my breath…. That's how I felt as Jim, Susan and I started on our drive to Fresno to meet Kirsten and Chris who would join Jim on this final triumphal segment of the amazing trek. Jim was determined to leave no segment untrekked—even though he knew the huge challenges that awaited him. But this time he would have a team. Even I did not appreciate how vital the team would be. I took them to the shuttle, then drove home to my other life for the days until my final retrieval trip.

I don't remember about the time at home; I just sit here picturing the cartons of journals and notes from those years that were donated to LA's recycle bins as another consequence of downsizing for the move. But I have vivid memories of the retrieval adventure about a week later…

On the day that would mark the conclusion of the hike, I drove to the designated area and sat in the car in the parking lot scouring the hillside for signs of familiar figures. As always, I looked at the surrounding foliage, studied the sky, watched other groups of hikers and thought about the memories—for some hours. And then I spotted Kirsten—the amazing Kirsten—striding, almost trotting–triumphantly down the hill with one of her glorious smiles. And Kirsten was followed by an unfamiliar young man. As I greeted K with hugs, she introduced the young man and explained that he was carrying Jim's pack, a favor that she had elicited to help her exhausted dad. I soon learned how exhausted Jim was….

But when Jim and the rest of the group came trudging down the trail, the overriding emotion was joy. He had made it!!! He had conquered that formidable piece of the high Sierras. He had met his own challenge and accomplished his goal. That was all that mattered.

As crazy and impossible as his plan had seemed to me when he had started this adventure, he had done it. And, over the years, we had figured out how we could collaborate to make it work. We had worked as a team, and that gave me satisfaction and joy. He had reached his goal, and, thanks to him, I also felt accomplished. The joy of partnership—what, for me, love is really about.

One of my favorite things to do is eat—especially in good company, so when the group decided to go out for a celebratory meal, I was ready. But Jim was not. Sleep was all he wanted. I was very concerned but decided to let him sleep and bring food to him. And he did manage to wake up and eat the bedside picnic when I returned. He would be okay—and he had triumphed. After a good night's sleep, we were ready to return to life in the city—with memories of a collaborative adventure that has further defined who we are as partners and as individuals. At this stage of our lives, that brings peace and satisfaction.

Sequel

Near the end of October Kirsten went to a book signing event in the San Francisco Bay Area for Bill Bryson's recent book, "At Home." She wanted to get his autograph for me, since his earlier book "A Walk in the Woods" had planted the seed for my decision to hike the PCT. Bryson signed her copy of his new book, and she told him briefly about her dad's hike. Then he signed the postcard she had brought which shows a map of the PCT. Bryson said, "Tell your dad I'm impressed!" Then he asked, "How long did it take him again?" She told him. Then, "And HOW old is he again?" She said "He'll be 76 in November." Bryson responded, "DEpressed! Tell your dad I'm DEpressed!" And they shared a good laugh.

Afterwords

So in America when the sun goes down and I sit on the old broken-down river pier watching the long, long skies over New Jersey and sense all that raw land that rolls in one unbelievable huge bulge over to the West Coast, and all that road going, all the people dreaming in the immensity of it... just before the coming of complete night that blesses the earth, darkens all rivers, cups the peaks and folds the final shore in, and nobody, nobody knows what's going to happen to anybody besides the forlorn rags of growing old...

JACK KEROUAC
ON THE ROAD

Reading an article about Kerouac's book *On the Road* started me ruminating about time and mortality. David Ulin, book critic for the Los Angeles Times, wrote "It took me years to understand what the book was getting at, which is the bittersweet ephemerality of everything, the idea that to 'know time' is to know ourselves as at time's mercy, which makes its frantic movement less exuberant than desperate." From Ulin's perspective, Kerouac presents his characters seeking experiences on the road trips in an inevitably futile quest to reckon with the threatened ravages of time, of mortality. Late in the novel the ancient hitchhiker tells young Sal (representing Kerouac) to "Go moan for man."

I met a rich variety of hikers on the trail seeking experiences of different sorts and for different reasons. Of particular interest to me were the ones who were out to hike a long distance. Many of the young hikers I talked with had just completed high school or college and had yet to begin their first career-oriented job or were about to begin a new job. They were taking advantage of a unique opportunity to spend several months on a grand adventure before launching into adulthood – or rather as an early step toward taking responsibility and beginning that phase of their lives. Hiking the PCT would be both an adventure and a memorable achievement. I was buoyed by their infectious enthusiasm. Whether they hiked the entire trail or not, this would be an achievement they could build on. I saw in their pursuit a welcome contrast to Kerouac's futile quest. Among these young hikers I did not sense any desperation about living fully before dying.

Other hikers I met were at different stages in life. Some who were in their forties or fifties told me about a different sort of life-changing point in their lives; for some, a crisis. Taking time out to hike this long trail was to give them an opportunity to think through complex changes or difficult realities they were facing, not always embracing. Careers, families, life goals, their very identities – most everything might be at stake. It seems to me now that for some of those hikers setting out on the trail was somewhat like Kerouac's going on the road, a rather desperate attempt to grapple with or escape or at least postpone facing what they feared. Many, of course, were simply intent on thinking through how they would deal with the challenges before them.

A small group of hikers I met was at a still later stage in life. Well-seasoned hikers or relative novices like myself in 2004, we were in our sixties and beyond. Retired or at least easing up on jobs and careers, some said they were simply hiking major sections of the PCT to enjoy a recreation which they now had more leisure to pursue. Many of us were seeking a unique adventure, and some a major achievement.

I set out to hike the PCT as a grand adventure in my rediscovered recreation of backpacking. But early on, once I had managed to hike over 100 miles on that first part of the trail, I also found that I had a sense of substantial accomplishment. My brother and I had hiked farther than anyone among our family or acquaintances had ever done. We had tried something which challenged us, and we succeeded.

Even with that sense of achievement, I found that actually completing my goal of hiking the whole trail from Mexico to Canada assumed increasing importance for me over the years of my adventure. I always knew I might break a leg or worse and be unable to complete the trail, as very nearly happened in 2008. The risks were real. I was getting older as well, and I had to accept and adjust to that reality along the way. But as early as 2005 I felt that I had proved to myself that I *could* do this feat. As I continued I grew more confident and determined that I *would* hike the whole trail, *"Lord willin' and the creek don't rise."*

By some important measures, Kerouac did not fare well in life. He wrote *On the Road* in his late 20's, so his fear of the ravages of growing old had begun early. His book was published six years later, and his ensuing fame was overwhelming. Kerouac died at the age of 47 of internal hemorrhaging due to his heavy drinking. The evidently desperate way he lived exacted a toll. He escaped growing old, but not without ravages of his own.

I am struck by the contrast between Kerouac's perspective in *On the Road* and my own perspective on the trail. While much older on the trail than Kerouac was on the road, I did not fear "the forlorn rags of growing old." Time could not threaten me in a fundamental way in the years of my hike, for I felt I had already lived fully. I married Zhita when I was the age at which Kerouac died. We are richly endowed with loved ones, with my two daughters, Zhita's two daughters, our grandkids and many more family and friends. By the time I retired and later set out on the Pacific Crest Trail, I had been living well for many years. I did not somehow earn or deserve all my good fortune, I am well aware. Many factors beyond my control made possible even being alive at my age and being the person I am. I'm a very lucky guy.

Utopia is not a dream that happens
in the future... utopia is
locating the golden age within the
boundaries of our own lives.

RENÉ MAGRITTE
IN A LETTER TO ANDRÉ BRETON
WRITTEN DURING THE RUINED AFTERMATH OF WORLD WAR II

Achieving my goal has been one of the most fulfilling experiences of my life. I had committed to long distance hiking in the wilderness, alone as well as with family and friends, and I had grown into the role. That was very satisfying. I also found that completing my goal further laid to rest my old disappointment about the unfinished dissertation - better still. Now I have even completed writing my story about the hike, enjoying that task from beginning to end and achieving yet another goal. The experiences of hiking the trail and then of writing the story all have been greatly enriched by my partnership with my wife; our shared experiences, in turn, contributed to our ever-developing relationship.

A further measure of my good fortune is that it was not until four years after I completed my hike that I was stricken with West Nile Virus. A year later I have progressed from hospital bed to wheelchair to walker, and I hope to continue to improve and someday be able to walk with a cane. This brings an end to my hiking – but I did complete my big hike.

Everyone knows that time will end for each of us. Kerouac was right about that. Even so, for many, a life seen as rich in experiences and relationships, perhaps seeking some worthy goals and benefitting other people, achieving a measure of success, however short of ideal, provides ample meaning and fulfillment. Knowing that our time will end need not preclude enjoyment and meaning in life. It strikes me now that writing one's story might serve to blur the finality of that final ending, in a sense extending one's presence beyond one's life. Too bad Kerouac found no comfort there.

Everyone should know that for each of us the end may arrive as we, our bodies, are very painfully "clothed in the forlorn rags of growing old." It seems Kerouac expected that for all. I may moan myself one day, everyone could say. That is an unwelcome prospect, and for some it may bring fear and a desperate scramble for experiences or achievements or escape. But I doubt that any of the hikers I met saw life as hopelessly overshadowed by the threat of potentially dying in misery someday. The possibility of an unpleasant end need not negate the value of one's life.

I have signed an Advance Directive to order no resuscitation or life support for me if my final stage of life is miserably painful or comatose and hopeless. Pull the plug. That is a practical remedy for a possible end. Not perfect, but good enough. That provided for, I can forget about it.

I have lived fully, and I've enjoyed my golden age.

...And I shall go. And the birds will go on singing...

JUAN RAMON JIMENEZ
THE FINAL JOURNEY

Footnote: A String of Pearls

I think of the long, thin line of the PCT as a string of pearls, featuring scene after lovely scene along its course. The Pacific Crest National Scenic Trail is a national treasure, offering access to mountains and plains, forests and deserts providing habitat for vegetation and wildlife relatively free of such human interventions as roadways and factories, logging and drilling. People are welcome as visitors, not residents.

Most of this string of pearls is protected by public ownership of the land on which the trail lies, land which is managed by public agencies sharing the vision of the Pacific Crest National Scenic Trail offering access to wilderness experiences. But there are weak spots in this string, parts of the trail which are on private land subject to development which would and sometimes already does mar the scenes we can observe from the trail. Even the public's right to walk on the trail is not permanently guaranteed. Nearly 200 miles of the PCT currently lie on private land, consisting of more than 1,500 tracts totaling more than 200,000 acres.

The Pacific Crest Trail Association is a nonprofit organization whose mission is to protect, preserve and promote the PCT. As the government's major partner in the operation of the trail, the PCTA has a "memorandum of understanding" with the U.S. Forest Service, the National Park Service, the Bureau of Land Management and California State

Parks to coordinate their roles in the management of the PCT. In addition to the work of maintaining the trail, the PCTA seeks to work with these agencies to secure permanent protection of threatened parts of the trail. Negotiations with the many willing sellers of land are hampered by lack of funds. The PCTA needs support in this mission.

I urge your support. For more information about the organization and how you can help, contact the PCTA at 1-888-PC-TRAIL or at www. pcta.org.

Annotated Bibliography

$\mathbf{G}$uinand, Maria *"Y se quedaran los pajaros cantando..."* (*"And the birds will go on singing..."*). 2009. Sheet music published by earthsongs. We heard this choral song performed by the Los Angeles Master Chorale, conducted for the occasion by Guinand on April 29, 2012. She said she had written the song based on the poem "El Viaje Definitivo" ("The Final Journey") by poet Juan Ramon Jimenez, who was awarded the Nobel Prize for Literature in 1956. On page 177 in "Afterwords" we quote the English translation of the first line of both the poem and the song as found in the sheet music.

Knight, Christopher. "Wait, you just lost me." **Los Angeles Times, Calendar** section, 27 December, 2012, p. 1. Knight, art critic of the Los Angeles Times, in a review of the art show "Lost (In LA)" at Barnsdall Park, wrote "One of the more enchanting objects on display is a 1946 letter... Belgian Surrealist Rene Magritte, writing to his friend Andre Breton... muses on the subject of utopia in the ruined aftermath of World War II. 'Utopia is not a dream that happens in the future,' Magritte observes, 'but utopia is *locating the golden age within the boundaries of our own lives.*' The emphasis is his, the handwritten words firmly underlined.

Both artists had by then survived two world wars." Our quote from the letter is on page 178 in "Afterwords"

Lampert, Ruth. "Love in the Sixties." **Voices**, journal of the American Academy of Psychotherapists, Summer 1993, p.60. Ruth wrote this article about meeting and marrying Tony Marolda when each of them was in their sixties. Tony joined her in coming to our book club meetings until they were well into their eighties. We quote her on page xv in "Retirement."

Rave, Karen. "A Killer temptation." Article special to the **Los Angeles Times, Fitness** section, 28 July 2008, p. F8. We quote from her article on page 80 in "2008 Rescue."

Ulin, David. "Not the same 'Road' or time," **Los Angeles Times, Calendar** section, 27 December, 2012, pp. 1,8. Ulin, book critic of the Los Angeles Times, wrote about Kerouac's book, **On the Road**, contrasting the message of the book with that of the movie based upon it. The movie focuses on the story's young people "driving, talking, smoking dope, listening to music…. [with] a kind of studied cool," as did Ulin when he read the book as a youth. But from a mature perspective Ulin sees the book expressing "the bittersweet ephemerality of everything, the idea that to 'know time' is to know ourselves as at time's mercy, which makes its frantic movement less exuberant than desperate." Ulin quotes the book's "magnificent closing paragraph," from which we excerpted the quote on page 173 in "Afterwords."

Ulin likened Kerouac's romantic view of what he experienced on the road to the views of many writers about their own experiences, and apropos of this point he cites Fitzgerald's pronouncement from the 1930's, which we quoted on page xiii.

Because of your melodic nature, the
moonlight never misses an appointment.
Lucky Numbers 11, 17, 22, 26, 31, 34

Our favorite Chinese cookie fortune, found in a fortune cookie at a
forgotten restaurant, quoted on page 79 in "2008 Rescue." (We did not
test the lucky numbers.)

*Every Sun that Rises, First Product of the Caddo Lake Oral History Project of East
Texas State University.* University of Texas Press, Austin, TX. 1985. p. 122.

Jim's Uncle John Pearson, brother-in-law of my mother, loved to
spend his annual vacation fishing in sprawling Caddo Lake in east Texas,
finding his way among the swamps and islands to return to his favorite
fishing holes each year. My brother John went on one of those trips,
where one day he found himself cleaning fish at the back of the boat and
unexpectedly feeding a water moccasin whose gaping mouth appeared
just inches from his hands. Uncle John let me read the oral history report where I found the following remarks by Wyatt Moore, one of those
interviewed for the oral history project. We quote from Moore on page
63 in "2007 Natural Beauty."

"Well, it's night on Taylor Island, and I'm looking at the moon and
waiting for the alligators to alligate and the hoot owls to hoot. It's a
wonderful world, ain't it? It's a wonderful world for them people that
is alive. I know a whole lots of people staggering around that is dead
as hell, don't see nothing, been dead most of their lives. Some people
never see a sunrise, or if they see it, never thought nothing about it. I
think every sun that rises done it just for me."

Appendix

First Aid Kit (A)	Survival Kit (B)	Daypack	Toiletries (C)	Front Pocket +
Moleskin	Compass	First Aid Kit(A)	Toothbrush	Trash Bag
1" Bandaids	Matches	Survival Kit(B)	Toothpaste	Guide Book
4x4 Pads	Candles	Nylon Line	Interdental	Maps
1/2" Tape	Whistle	Headlamp	Refills	Permits *Journal*
Gauze	Duct Tape	Rain Jacket	Floss	Filter Info
2" Elastic wrap	Space Blanket	Satellite Phone*	Vitamins, etc.	Stove Info
Second Skin	Water Purifier	Water Bag	Nail File	Trowel
Wipes	Toilet Paper	Water Tube	Nail Clippers	Toilet Paper
Tylenol	*3 mil ...*	Chess Set*	Spoon	Fuel Bottle
Sunscreen		*Ear Plug*	Journal	Toiletries(C)
Tweezers			Pen	Water Filter
Safety pins			Bladder Cap	
Immodium			Soap	
Cough drops		*seal seams*	Sunscreen	
Ointment			Repellant	
Knife w/scissors			Lip Balm	
Iodine			Glasses Wipe	
Field Guide			Cough Drops	
Desitin*			Wipes	
Petroleum Jelly			Ear Plugs*	
			Comb	
			Wire Ties	

Clothes Bag (D)	Cookset Bag (E)	Main Pack	Outside	Wear/Suitcase
2 (3) Pr. Socks	Stove	Air Mattress	Water Bottle	Watch, Compass
2 (3) Pr. Underwear	Lighter	Clothes Bag(D)	Snacks	Underwear
‡ (2) Bandanas	Accessories	Cocoon*	Camera	Whistle, Light
Sun Hat	Windscreen	Rain Pants*	Bandana	Socks *briefs*
Laundry Bag	Pot & Lid	Water Shoes	Tent	Pants
Long Underwear*	Gripper	Fleece*	Footprint	Shirt
Gloves*		Cookset(E)	GPS*	Boots
Warm Hat*		Mug	Poles	Hat
Wash Cloths		P Bottle	*Petroleum jelly*	Sunglasses
Rinse Cloth		Food Bag (G)		Wallet (F)
		Sleeping Bag		Knife
		Trash Bag		Pen
				Sandals
				Bandana

Fishing*	Cooking*	Wallet (F)	Food Bag (G)	
Pole	Skillet	Kaiser copy	Dinners	
Reel, Line	Spatula	Hike Permit	Olive Oil	Extra Food
Hooks	Olive Oil	Fire Permit	Energy Bars	
Sinkers	Salt, Pepper	Cash	Meat	
Lures	Garlic Powder	Credit Card	Starch/Veggie	
Salmon Eggs	Detergent	Golden Age P.	Nuts	
Stringer	Scrubber	Address & Phone	Fruit	
Fishing License		ATM Card	Chocolate	
		Drivers License*	Drink Mixes	

Bear bag

185

Revised PCT Hike 2008   8/7/2008

Date	S > N	Destination	Elevation Changes	Elevation	Miles drive/hike	Totals
8-Aug		**Drive to San Rafael**			d400	
9-Aug		**Drive to Oroville, Yreka**			d370	
10-Aug	1674.7	Horse Camp Trail	4530	5900	d50 12.6	
11-Aug	1690	junction Alex Hole Camp	-1130,+1860	6630	15.3	
12-Aug	1705.5	Wrangle Gap	-1300,+1720,-500	6500	15.5	
13-Aug	1721.2	Ashland Inn **Zhita**	-1700,+1200,-1500	5500	15.7	
14-Aug	1738.3	spring-fed tub	-1250,+1300	5550	17.1	
15-Aug	1750.2	Hyatt Lake Road	-1000,+400,-300,+400	5090	11.9	
16-Aug		**Day off, Ashland**				88.1
17-Aug	1762.8	Griffen Pass Road	+450,-650,+1200	5640	12.6	
18-Aug	1780.4	Fish Lake Trail	+550,-1250	4940	17.6	
19-Aug	1794.5	Red Lake Trail	+1300,-300	6020	14.1	
20-Aug	1810.1	Honeymoon Creek	+1300,-1300	5980	15.6	
21-Aug	1825.2	old road	-200,+600,-300,+250	6290	15.1	
22-Aug	1841	Rim Drive	+,-,+1520,-900	6510	15.8	
23-Aug		**Day off, Crater Lake**				90.6
24-Aug	1853.5	Hwy 138 +	-1700	5935	12.5	
25-Aug	1868.4	past Tipsoo Peak	+1450,-400,+600,-300	7200	14.9	
26-Aug	1882.9	Cascade Lakes Road	-1000,+,-300,+400,-800	5820	14.5	
27-Aug	1900.4	up a switchback, ponds	+1300,-1550,+1000	6560	17.5	
28-Aug	1916.9	North Rosary Lake	-1560,+830	5830	16.5	
29-Aug	1931	Road 5897, Charlton Lake	+350,-700,+900,-500	5840 d60	14.1	
30-Aug		**Day off, Eugene**				90.0
31-Aug	1940.7	Stormy Lake	-300,+500	6045 d60	9.7	
1-Sep	1952.4	Dumbbell Lake	-1000,+460	5500	11.7	
2-Sep	1964.3	Sisters Mirror Lake	+160,-400,+700	5980	11.9	
3-Sep	1977.4	Obsidian Trail	+230,-500,+760	6380	13.1	
4-Sep	1989.5	McKenzie Highway 242	+270,-630	5280 d70	12.1	
5-Sep		**Day off, Eugene**				58.5
6-Sep	2004.9	Lilypad Pond	+900,-800,+400,-1000	4790 d70	15.4	
7-Sep	2020.8	Rockpile Lake	+1690,-1150,+900	6250	15.9	
8-Sep	2034.2	Milk Creek	+150,-1080	4320	13.4	
9-Sep	2050.7	Upper Lake	+1600,-90,+1000,-1560	5380	16.5	
10-Sep	2053.2	**Skyline Rd 42 Olallie Lake**	-400	4990 d110	2.5	
	2063.4	Trooper Springs Junction	-600	4400	10.2	
11-Sep	2074	Warm Springs River	+600,-1700	3300	10.6	
12-Sep	2083.4	Skyline Road 42	+930,-860	3370 d130	9.6	
13-Sep		**Day off, Eugene**				94.1
14-Sep		**Williams**			d420	
15-Sep		**San Francisco**			d125	
16-Sep		**Home**			d400	
						421.5

186

Made in the USA
San Bernardino, CA
16 April 2017